Louisiana Haunted Forts

Louisiana Haunted Forts

Elaine Coleman

TAYLOR TRADE PUBLISHING
Lanham • New York • Dallas • Boulder • Toronto • Oxford

Published by Taylor Trade Publishing
An imprint of The Rowman & Littlefield Publishing Group, Inc.
4501 Forbes Boulevard, Suite 200, Lanham, Maryland 20706

Distributed by NATIONAL BOOK NETWORK

Library of Congress Cataloging-in-Publication Data

Coleman, Elaine.
  Louisiana haunted forts / by Elaine Coleman.
     p. cm.
  Includes bibliographical references and index.
     ISBN 978-1-58979-239-5 (pbk. : alk. paper)
1. Fortification-Louisiana-History-Anecdotes. 2. Haunted places-Louisiana-
Anecdotes. 3. Historic sites-Louisiana-Anecdotes. 4. Ghosts-Louisiana-
Anecdotes. 5. Louisiana-History, Local-Anecdotes. 6. Louisiana-Biography-
Anecdotes. I. Title.
  F370.C57 2005
  976.3-dc22

                                                               2005009318

∞™ The paper used in this publication meets the minimum requirements of
American National Standard for Information Sciences-Permanence of Paper
for Printed Library Materials, ANSI/NISO 239.48-1992.

This book is dedicated to my husband Jerry. He has been so patient throughout the research and writing of this book.

CONTENTS

FOREWORD

Ghost stories are as much a part of America's landscape as the military forts built upon it in the nineteenth century. They speak of legends marking the lives and deaths of courageous men and women. These stories impart an understanding about the nature of good and evil, about what can happen when raw emotions, clamorous events, and violent reactions are heaped together. A ghostly tale teaches us to be cautious while it raises the hairs on the backs of our necks.

Elaine Coleman's *Louisiana Haunted Forts* scrapes at the heart of history and offers a trove of ghostly tales fit to tell around a campfire on many a dark night. Take, for instance, the tale of vengeance surrounding the apparition of a Confederate soldier seen by taxi driver Thomas Jenkins as he was driving near Fort Turnbull. This could be just another ghost sighting. In Elaine's hands, though, the reader senses the fear and hopelessness of soldiers who must fight in "eyeball range" of the enemy. You understand the bravery it took to defend the land. You know the reason why the spirit of Johnny Franks returns night after night on the lonely road that led to his untimely death one hundred and fifty years ago.

Elaine moves the reader from cold foggy evenings to strange, clammy cold spots found in such locales as Fort St. Jean Baptiste. Many of the fort's reenactors claim that odd visitors will show up during their tours, dressed in period clothing and, more often than not, in some amount of distress. There's the story of the beautiful African woman who is seen crying as she asks where her children are. The guides have also noticed Louis Antoine Juchereau de St. Denis prowling the grounds. St. Denis spent his life at Fort St. Jean Baptiste, and rumor has it he is buried beneath the floorboards of the old church. His ghostly appearance makes one think he's there to watch over the day-to-day activities of the fort.

This book is more than the telling of tales. While it introduces you to the ghosts of Louisiana, it uncovers the creation of a nation. It will also make you want to explore modern ghost-busting on its own merits to see what you can find out. For her part, Elaine is an expert at finding lurking apparitions and coaxing them to share their stories. So, come along, and don't be scared!

Denise Vitola
Author of the Ty Merrick Mysteries

ACKNOWLEDGMENTS

I would like to say thank you to the folks at the Louisiana State Parks Service. They never failed to answer my questions or to send me to someone who could. I certainly appreciate their help. To all the people I called on for stories from the different areas of the state, I say thank you. Thank you to Frankie Bertrand; Gwen Dardar; J. A. Allen; Andy and Tom Adkins; Ilse Fisher; Clay Carter; Steve Bounds, manager at the Mansfield Battlefield Historical Site; and Steve Mayeux with the Friends of Fort DeRussy, some of those with whom I talked on the phone at the forts and about photos. You have all been great friends to me in this project. To the taxi driver, Don Woodard, who chauffeured Jerry and me around Shreveport, thank you. We explored places even he didn't know about.

I also want to say thank you to Dixie and Desmond Powell, Joanne (Sammy) Horn, Donnie Burks, Barbara Rollins, Sue Turner, Gwen Choate, Robyn O'Brien, Nancy Masters, Pansy Mallow, and Denise Vitola. You all are my cheering section, and I love you. To Janet Harris, thank you is not enough for me to say how I feel about the way you have helped me make this book the best it could be.

INTRODUCTION

My fascination with ghosts and spirits began as a child at my Aunt Pearl's knee. She told ghost stories to me while I was doing her fingernails.

My father moved our family to the country in 1972. While he worked nights, my mother, brother, sister, and I sat around the fireplace with the lights off, telling ghost stories until bedtime. Some nights we drove away from the house, down the lane where trees overlapped above us, and told more scary stories.

Up in the pasture I found a cave, and I explored that hole in the mountain wall many times. I discovered shards of pottery, an old spoon, and other relics of the past along with Belle Starr's name carved into the wall. I imagined the lady outlaw's ghost surely lived in the cave. I hoped that someday her ghost might speak to me. At times I waited for hours.

Once, on New Year's Eve, my friends and I visited an old Indian cemetery. We witnessed a blue light floating behind us. We left in a hurry. I wanted to return to see who didn't want us there, but my friends were afraid.

The legends that make up our heritage are sometimes fact and sometimes fiction. I have often craved the ability to speak to ghosts from the past. I feel that through my study of history, I've possessed that ability to an extent. These cravings for information have helped me on my quest to separate fact from legend. I hope that the stories within these pages are an equal mixture of both.

Elaine Coleman

I

Sportsman's Paradise

Fort Turnbull/Fort Humbug

The Post at Ouachita/Fort Miro

Camp Boggs

Fort Johnston

Fort Smith

1

FORT TURNBULL/FORT HUMBUG

An eerie dense fog draped over the monument of Old Fort Turnbull. A rattletrap taxi slowed to a crawl. Driving slowly through the fog, Thomas Jenkins slammed on the brakes, narrowly avoiding a figure in the street. He honked his horn a couple of times. A young man dressed in Confederate gear smiled at Jenkins and waved. Jenkins stepped from his taxi to confront the young man. He walked toward the young man and halted abruptly. The chill in the air took him by surprise. He shivered.

A loud blast from somewhere in the night momentarily drew his attention. He turned back to the young man and saw no one. The fog lifted. Jenkins hurried back to his vehicle. In the seat lay a Confederate cap, tattered and torn. When he picked up the cap, his fingers became extremely cold for a few seconds. Another blast and Jenkins sped from the monument, clutching the cap.

Thomas Jenkins never fails to honk as he drives past the Fort Turnbull/Humbug Armory and the fake cannon standing as a monument to the old fort. After relating his story of the man in the fog to his comrades, Jenkins learned the real story behind the young man and the cap.

Johnny Franks was a fifteen-year-old boy who wanted badly to avenge both his brothers' deaths. They had left to fight for the life and land they loved with the Confederate troops. His mother was adamant that he was too young to join them. She didn't want to lose her youngest son to the war as well.

Unknown to her, one night when the fog rolled across the land from the Red River, Johnny Franks slipped from the family home. He donned the tattered cap and coat that had belonged to one of his brothers. His first stop was Fort Turnbull. He and other men in the city, along with approximately nine hundred slaves, had worked side-by-side to get the dirt entrenchments built earlier in the year. Johnny had been amazed at the way the men of Shreveport had pulled together. Men of wealth and those like his parents, not so wealthy, as well as the slaves and even soldiers, worked to build Fort Turnbull. They were determined not to allow Shreveport to become another disaster like Vicksburg. He'd been proud to be a part of such an ingenious line of fortifications that were to surround the capital city of Louisiana. Johnny and his father had even sat in on the meeting with General Kirby E. Smith. The governors of Louisiana, Texas, Arkansas, and Missouri also attended.

He hadn't particularly understood all the discussions that took place, but he knew all about the fall of Vicksburg and the Battle of Gettysburg. Johnny knew Fort Turnbull would serve as only one of the forts in a chain.

They'd need him to help fight General Banks's Yankee soldiers. His mother would just have to understand and let him join. If she didn't, well, he figured he was old enough to make that decision. When he and his friends whipped the Union invaders, he'd come home, and his mother would be proud of his heroism.

Johnny and many of his friends used their fathers' tools to help build Fort Turnbull, and they all wanted to be a part of the army. One other of the boys had become good at sneaking out of the house at night. Sometimes they went out to hunt or hide and listen to the meetings of adults. One day soon after Fort Turnbull was finished, he left the house just at dusk and headed straight for the fort. He was supposed to meet his friend, and they were going to stand guard outside of the fort. That particular night, for reasons Johnny never found out, Hank never showed up at the fort. Johnny wore the cap and coat he had stashed in the barn. In them, he was a Confederate soldier.

Crouching low against the dirt wall, Johnny shivered. He fell asleep at his self-appointed post at the base of the dirt wall, dreaming of being a soldier. A dense fog enveloped the earth as he slept. Just after midnight, he awakened and pulled his coat closer around his thin young chest. Unafraid, Johnny stood and started home.

A voice from the thick fog called out for Johnny to halt. Friendly as ever, he started to wave. The person behind the voice, fearing assault, fired his weapon at the dead center of Johnny's heart. He fell to his knees, a smile stuck on his face. A second shot hit Johnny in the shoulder. He fell forward, his hand in a permanent waving position. Johnny Franks, a young man who wanted to fight for his family and land, died on that cold foggy night in 1864. He never achieved his dream of joining the Confederate Army, but he continues to guard Fort Humbug.

Shreveport is not threatened today, but it needed to be protected in the days of the Civil War. General N. P. Banks planned to attack the capital city. General Banks's men were the ones who killed Johnny's brothers. Banks was supposed to be coming to Shreveport from Alexandria.

The officers who came up with the plans for the forts surrounding Shreveport felt that attacks on Shreveport were almost impossible because of the swamps and the malaria that hovered over the waters surrounding the city. After all, malaria was something everyone was frightened of in the summer months. However, the officials of Shreveport didn't think the Red River and its forests would be enough to stop General Banks. Not even the natural blockage of the "Red River Raft" would be able to stop the Yankees if they attacked. The Yankees could figure out how to get past the fallen trees and other blockage that clogged the river. Many people had ridden their horses right across all the brush at low spots in the river—although navigating the brush and sludge had proved to be suicide for some.

The modern-day Louisiana National Guard Armory sits on part of the property where Fort Humbug, formerly known as Fort Turnbull, lies at rest. Because of a conversation with General Kirby E. Smith in 1864, General McGruder renamed the post "Fort Humbug."

"But General, you and I both know we are fighting a war of 'eyeball range' and mostly by feel."

With less than five cannons in the area, the officers didn't have enough fire power to hold off Banks and his troops. According to legend, the officers thought they'd help the Confederate cause by using "Quaker guns." However, General McGruder was not impressed with the way General Smith handled the situation.

"Man, I'm telling you there's no way a bunch of burned logs that you hope will look like cannons are going to fool General Banks."

General Smith believed that with a two hundred-yard-wide river to be crossed and with the fake guns placed just right, it would give the Yankee general the impression that the Confederate Army had a hardy defense in store for him. He felt General Banks would think twice before he tried an attack on Fort Turnbull.

General McGruder assured Smith he hoped he was right, but he didn't think anyone could fool the Union army with fake cannons. "Your forts are nothing but a humbug," he told Smith.

The name has remained throughout history. Adjacent to the Armory is the Overton Brooks V.A. Medical Center. It, too, proudly sits atop the old historic fort. Some of the old log ramparts and earthen breastworks remain. Some of them are inside the fence that surrounds the National Guard headquarters.

The "Quaker gun" that sits in front of the gates at Fort Humbug.

The *Shreveport Times* ran an article about the soldiers from Fort Humbug after the September 11, 2001, terrorist attacks. As the soldiers prepared to head home at night, people passing by would honk and wave. Some say it was an outpouring of support for our soldiers absent since Desert Storm.

Are they honking at the soldiers of today or at Johnny Franks, who never really became a soldier?

Fort Humbug is prepared for war now. It hasn't been this busy since World War II or since the chaotic times when it was established in 1864. If visitors were to drive by late in the evening and look closely, especially if the fog has rolled in from the Red River, they might be able to see Johnny Franks. If taking a taxi, a visitor might be riding with a man who has seen Johnny Franks at the Fort Humbug cannon monument and the state plaque.

Visitors driving around Shreveport at night should be able to see, off in the distance, a large star-shaped light shining down on the remains of Fort Turnbull/Fort Humbug. The fort lies quietly between Stoner Avenue and Clyde Fant Memorial Parkway. Entrance to the Fort Humbug Memorial Park can be easily found from Fant and Youree streets. The "Quaker gun" stands on the corner. At the end of the avenue is the dismantled park, the concrete foundations of which are all that remain, just beside Stoner Av-

The front of the National Guard building that is still named Fort Humbug.

enue. Walkways have been built between some of the embankments and are still used by the public.

Fort Turnbull is manned today by National Guardsmen who protect us at home and abroad. But there is one guard left over from the Civil War days who stands near the old cannon out front. Johnnie Franks has been seen guarding the fort in his Rebel uniform.

2

THE POST AT
OUACHITA/FORT MIRO

James, who works at the Monroe courthouse, needed to do some week-end work and went to his office downtown late one Saturday afternoon. The courthouse sits on the banks of the Ouachita River. James knew the history of the area very well. However, he wasn't prepared in the least for what met him at the office that day.

James often worked weekends. On this afternoon, his mind strayed from his work. From time to time he caught himself staring out the window. He leaned back in his chair and closed his eyes for a moment. A chill filled the room and he pulled his jacket closer around his chest, but the cold increased. Shivering, he went to adjust the thermostat. He stopped in his tracks as he heard sounds of fighting outside his office. He listened closer. As the noises grew and the temperature continued to drop, the scene un-folding before him sickened him. Men with lances and muskets were killing each other. Women and children were also being killed before his eyes. Cries of fear and death filled his ears. At the time he didn't realize what he was witnessing. He rubbed his eyes in an attempt to make the vision disap-pear. Running from the room, he began searching for a television and VCR. He even tried to find a hidden projector. He found nothing. Hurrying from room to room, he searched down the halls and in other offices for the source of the horrible scene.

James returned to his office. He found no traces of the massacre scene. The room was back to its normal temperature. Unnerved at the lack of proof of what he'd just witnessed, he fidgeted at his desk. He thumbed through the papers lying there, continually thinking about what he'd seen. Who were the men doing the killing? Who was being murdered? The dead all seemed to be settlers, and the murderers were apparently Natchez Indi-ans. He had witnessed a massacre, but who were they?

The longer he sat at the desk, the more he thought about what he'd seen. Suddenly a putrid odor filled the office. Becoming ill, James felt his stomach churn. The smells grew worse. Decay and the scent of death circulated throughout his office. Moans of pain emanated from the walls. He grabbed his keys and left the office in a hurry.

Weeks of work and no sleep took their toll. James couldn't forget what he saw. The memory of the odors and the cold temperatures haunted him day and night. Every time he closed his eyes, the scene eased into his dreams and kept him awake. No matter how determined he was, the massacre scene came back time after time. Regardless of whether he was at the courthouse or home, the scenes played out, especially when he was near the Ouachita River. James eventually left Monroe but says he still sees the massacre in his mind.

The Post at Ouachita began because of the Natchez Massacre in 1729. The warring Natchez Indians killed any and all in their path. Men, women, and children were tortured and killed or left to die. The French settlers and friendly Indians moved eastward toward the Mississippi River for better protection. The Post at Ouachita was also moved eastward and was later established again in 1791. This event led to the settlement of Fort Miro and eventually the city of Monroe. After the Natchez Massacre in 1729, all settlements near the Ouachita River were abandoned. Only trappers and Indian traders ventured along the Ouachita and in De Siard and Bartholomew Bayous during the French era. The French planned no settlements or permanent structures during their reign in the Ouachita territory. The French simply survived with the Indians as best they could.

The Spanish rule came to the Ouachita River around 1774. Governor Miro and Don Juan Filhiol, originally French, were given large land grants by the Spanish, if they met certain criteria. They helped to establish Spanish rule in the area as early as 1780. After about five years, Filhiol decided that the settlement was too far out into the wilderness and moved the fort down the Ouachita River to Prairies des Canots. The fort was first known as the Post at Ouachita. Early in 1790, a number of settlers petitioned Don Juan Filhiol to build a fort. The settlers claimed they needed the fort for protection from the hostile Indians in the area. Later in the year, he decided to build a stockade. That way, the settlers would have a place to congregate if the Indians attacked.

In 1792, Governor Carondelet sent a military report to his superiors referring to Fort Ouachita. He reported that the fort consisted of only a few palisades. According to his description, the fort was directly in front of

Natchez. The inhabitants of the fort were fully responsible for its upkeep and design. Governor Carondelet and the Spanish took over the fort and later abandoned the original site.

In 1796, the fort was moved to the site of Fort Miro. Fort Miro was garrisoned by a sergeant and fifteen foot soldiers. Originally there were to be twenty families, but the men in charge failed to bring those families to the territory. Later, in violation of the agreement with the Spanish government, only a group of single men was living in the settlement. Families were supposed to be living in the settlement, not single men. The United States maneuvered troops into position to attack the Spanish fortress in 1797, because of a slight disagreement between the two countries. Then the Spanish abandoned the fort. The planned attack never was carried out. At the end of the eighteenth century, a prison was built at Ouachita Point near Monroe.

A surveyor was to be sent to start work on the new fort. He didn't arrive until December 1802, and the survey was not completed until January 1803, after the Spanish Marquis's death. Soon afterward, the United States purchased the Louisiana Territory and all the military establishments.

On January 31, 1804, General Wilkinson sent half a company of troops to take over the Post of Ouachita. This fort was located on the Black River, or Washatau. The Spanish were holding the grounds under the command of a junior officer, Lieutenant Joseph Bowmar. Bowmar surrendered the fort to General Wilkinson, and the United States took possession of the fort on April 15, 1804.

Lieutenant Bowmar had enclosed several crude houses with a flimsy stockade. The pickets were spaced too far apart, and there was no cannon protection for the post. William Durbar and George Hunter toured the Post at Ouachita in November of 1804. This post was located approximately four hundred yards downstream from the original Fort Miro, which had been torn down and abandoned. In October 1804, nineteen American soldiers occupied the post. These men stayed at Fort Miro until 1808.

Upon the purchase of the Louisiana Territory, the U. S. government began dividing the territory states and Louisiana into parishes. By 1854, the area between and including Monroe and Bayou De Siard was shown on a map of the Shreveport and Texas Railroad. The railroad divided Monroe down the middle.

The Spanish fort was at the village of Prairie des Canots in 1785 and is now present-day Monroe, renamed in 1819. The site of the old fort is near South Grant Street between Calyso and Oak Streets. The American log stockade known as the Post at Ouachita from 1804 to 1808 was located some four hundred yards south of the old Spanish fort. There is nothing left of Fort Miro except perhaps the spirits of the men who fought the Natchez Indians to protect their women and children. The Natchez Indians massacred the settlers along the Ouachita River. The spirits of those who died must surely haunt the parts of Monroe along South Grant Street.

3

CAMP BOGGS

Camp Boggs was used to hold prisoners from the war and other walks of life. Prisoners of war were often treated badly. A large percentage of soldiers sent to prison camps died. The Union and Confederate prison camps were no place to be if ill or wounded. There were few doctors to be found during the Civil War. Those doctors who served on either side of the war had little to work with in the way of medications. However, the Confederate doctors were even more hindered by the lack of supplies than their Union counterparts.

Marsha lived near where Camp Boggs once stood. Her home was only about a quarter of a mile from the prison site. Marsha lived alone and worked in Shreveport. One evening as she drove into her driveway from work, she noticed a bright bouncing orb near a yard ornament close to the boundary of her property. She parked in the driveway and sat for a few minutes watching the strange light as it bounced here and there. It didn't seem to have any certain pattern or path to follow. As dusk turned to darkness, Marsha took out her flashlight and started toward the light. As she pointed the beam of the flashlight toward the eerie bouncing orb, it stopped moving and faded into the darkness for a few minutes.

Marsha called her German shepherd, put on his leash, and led him toward where she first saw the orb. Her dog tried to get away and go back to the garage. He fought the leash and circled her legs several times. She held tight to the leash and searched for the orb. She found nothing. After putting the dog back in the garage, she went back to where she saw the orb. As she searched the fence line for some source of light, she felt a deep coldness creep over her. The summer night suddenly became very cold, and the orb appeared once more at the same spot it had disappeared. It bounced around the perimeter of her yard, in and around the same place she saw it before.

Marsha hurried into the house and didn't go out into the yard again that night but watched the light for several hours from her kitchen window.

The next morning, Marsha once again investigated the spot where she had seen the strange light. She found no evidence of anything out of the ordinary, nor did she find footprints or any other sign that someone had been outside her yard playing tricks on her. Puzzled, Marsha went to work. That evening as she returned, the orb once again bounced around in the growing dusk. Marsha walked toward it. The orb moved in a circle until she reached the fence line. As she stood near the fence, the orb hovered just above the ground. Minutes passed as she stood watching it. The orb became elongated and began spreading upward. The filmy airy orb took on the shape of a man. Moments later, a soldier, bloody and dirty, stood at the fence reaching out to her. The spirit's hands shook, and the moan of pain it uttered shook her soul.

Marsha reached out her hand to touch the spirit's chest, where blood oozed from a bullet wound. The coldness she felt caused her to shiver. Being a nurse, she had seen many bullet wounds. Nothing she'd ever seen had prepared her for this victim. She wanted to help the man but wondered how she could help a spirit. The soldier began to cry and faded into the night. For several nights in a row, the orb appeared. Each time, Marsha went to the fence; every time, the orb took the shape of a dying soldier. Each time as she wondered what she could do to comfort him, the soldier disappeared, crying and reaching out to her for help.

For the past five years, this has happened in the same phase of the moon in June. Marsha still wonders how to help this spirit rest in peace. She has expanded her property, and since that time, the soldier seems to be less restless, staying around for only a night or two at a time.

Today there are no remains of Camp Boggs left to view. In 1864, the fort originally sat about a mile and a half south of Shreveport, on what is now private property. The Confederate camp was named for General Kirby Smith's chief of staff, Boggs. It was occupied by the 3rd Louisiana Infantry Regiment, later replaced by the 24th Regiment, sometimes called the "Crescent." These Confederate soldiers held their positions from August 15, 1864, when Camp Boggs was built, until the end of the Civil War.

Initially, Camp Boggs was only a tent camp in an open field out of Shreveport. As the weather became colder, the soldiers were ordered to build more permanent shelters. The tents came down, and the soldiers began work on the fortress walls and buildings. Camp Boggs was constructed of heavy oak timbers. The timbers were driven into the ground to form the perimeters. The fort was basically used to contain prisoners of war as well as other locals from Shreveport and the surrounding area who disobeyed the law. Often, runaway slaves were detained there.

The soldiers who still roam the private property of old Camp Boggs must have been prisoners of war. Perhaps they want to finish their lives and make good out of their bad situations in the past. Marsha lives inside a large fenced area and waits for the orb to appear. Some of her nights are spent watching the light from inside her home. Other nights she stands in front of the spirit, wishing she could help.

4

FORT JOHNSTON

An occasional high-pitched squeal of delight rings out across the playground on North Western Street in Shreveport. Other times the sound of bugles that call an end to the day can be heard in the lonely, isolated city park. No bugler can be seen to play "Taps" through the twilight hours. As dusk turns to darkness, all is quiet again.

Marie took her son to play at the old city park and sat on a bench watching him. She shivered when an extra-cold breeze wafted over the park. What she saw and heard next caused her to have several sleepless nights. The gaunt faces of the men who marched out of the brush frightened her. The men who came toward her and her son were totally transparent. However, she could see the uniforms they wore clear as day. The blood stains glowed as if on fire. One of the men in the group put a bugle to his filmy lips and began to blow into the instrument. At first, the sound was low and sounded as if someone were moaning in pain. The longer he stood blowing the horn, the louder the sound became. She wasn't the only one who heard the noises. Her six-year-old son has talked nonstop about the soldier man blowing the bugle. He described the gray coat the man was wearing, a Confederate infantry soldier's uniform.

The boy told his mother the man just stood in the park and played pretty music on the shiny bugle. He said the man liked to play the bugle. The boy also told his mother that the man had even talked to him sometimes when she wasn't looking. This frightened her even more. She discontinued their visits to the park for a while. The child begged to return and she asked why.

"I like to watch for the man with the horn," he says. "I don't like the other men."

Marie says she shivers every time her son tells her what he saw. When she compared what her son told her with everything she saw, she said she never wanted to return to the park. She said that not only did she see the bugler and the group of soldiers, but she also saw one of the marching soldiers stumble and fall forward. He grabbed at his chest and knocked down the man in front of him. She couldn't believe her eyes. When one of the other men turned the soldier onto his back, a huge blood stain covered his tattered uniform. She rushed to help him and nearly knocked her son to the ground. When she looked back at the soldier, he began to fade out of sight. Her son pointed and asked where the man in the gray coat went. Again, she looked where the man had been, and there was nothing. She took her son firmly by the hand and quickly left the park.

Weeks later, Marie's curiosity got the best of her. She returned to the city park alone. She waited. Just at twilight the scenario began to develop, and the sound of "Taps" played loud and clear. The marching soldiers slowed their steps. The horrible incident took place again. The soldier fell and was turned over to reveal the bloody coat and pleading eyes. Again, she stepped forward to try to help. She wrinkled her nose as the pungent odor of death and decay assaulted her nostrils. She pressed forward. As she approached the fallen man, she grew extremely cold in the heat of the summer night. The soldiers surrounded her as she reached to touch the injured man. When she reached down to the soldier on the ground, nothing but dust came in contact with her hand. The freezing cold she'd felt moments before faded slowly, and the putrid smell of death dissipated as well. Marie never took her son to the park again.

Fort Johnston, named for Albert Sidney Johnston, stood at the edge of Shreveport. It was only one of the forts built by slave labor to protect Shreveport and Cane City, now known as Bossier City. The entrenchments and forts were erected so they encircled Shreveport. The slave laborers who built the forts came from the plantations of the surrounding areas. Citizens of the city and the soldiers themselves worked alongside the slaves to dig the ditches used as fortifications.

Built farther north from Shreveport than the other three major forts in the area, Fort Johnston was the smallest. The fort was also the westernmost fort of the Shreveport defenses. The fort's purpose was to help keep attackers from coming downriver and attacking Shreveport from behind. Logically, an attack on the city would come from gunboats on the river and foot soldiers marching on the driest ground they could find.

Once the fort was built to the satisfaction of the officers in charge, the slaves were sent back to their plantations, and the citizens went back to their homes.

The soldiers stationed at the fort had daily routines they followed. They practiced day and night. They had to learn what to do if Yankee General Banks and his men attacked. In the mornings they marched and practiced. In the evenings, they marched and practiced as well. There were only a few men at each of the Shreveport forts, but they were good men and wanted to defend the city at all costs. One young soldier in particular had come home to the South from his schooling in the North when the fighting broke out and war was declared. He had been studying music but thought that his homeland needed him. Thomas was not a violent man, but he knew where his duty lay. He brought his bugle with him, and he entertained the men at Fort Johnston when he wasn't blaring out the audible orders on the horn. He practiced with the other men. As they marched, he blew his horn for them to march by. He greeted the day with his bugle, and he ended the day with it as well. Thomas's father was also stationed at Fort Johnston. Thomas was his only child.

Late one evening, Thomas played while his father marched with the other men to take the flag down and put it away for the night. When they were about halfway to the flag pole, a loud crack resounded across the darkening sky. Thomas's father grabbed his chest and fell to the ground. Thomas ran to help him, but the older man's eyes were fixed in death. Tears trickled down Thomas's cheeks as he began to sound "Taps" on the bugle for the last time. The men at Fort Johnston commented that the bugle sounded as if it were moaning in pain. The next morning, Thomas was found dead in his blanket for no apparent reason. His buddies said it was from a broken heart. He had lost his mother a year to the day that he lost his father. They said he couldn't stand being in the war. His father's violent death broke his heart. The bullet that hit his father was a stray from someone cleaning a gun, a pure and simple accident.

The soldiers continued without Thomas, but the mornings were not the same, and neither were the nights. They all practiced so that they could keep the Union soldiers from attacking Fort Johnston, but they did it with a lot less enthusiasm after the death of one of Shreveport's younger citizens. Sometimes in the evening, soldiers at the fort continued to hear "Taps" carried along on the wind.

Fort Johnston was built to keep the Union Army away from Shreveport and her citizens. Each fort on the defense line used four cannons aimed at pre-sited points where the gunboats would possibly come up the river. The fort could also rob the Yankee infantrymen of their cover. Fort Johnston was built along a marshy area to keep the Union infantry in swampy waters. Because of its position on the line of defense, Fort Johnston was touted as the most important in the defense line.

In 1864, Shreveport was the Trans-Mississippi capital and had to be protected at all costs. Other forts in this line of defense included Fort Jenkins, facing the south, and Battery Ewell, on the east side of the Red River, facing west.

Fort Johnston is one of the best preserved of the seventeen defenses because progress hasn't taken a toll on the earthen breastworks that were built all those years ago. Thanks to its position within an old city park, it remained relatively undisturbed through generations, neglected and overlooked.

Breastworks of Fort Johnston can be found in and around a recently semi-developed playground. It is about a half-block down North Western Street, off Caddo Street, near downtown Shreveport. Surrounding the site of the small playground are older homes built on top of the breastworks, and in the trenches of the breastworks are the streets. The playground is at the edge of a wooded area of earthen mounds and trenches where Fort Johnston once protected the citizens of Shreveport. The trees and brush which now cover the site were not there during the Civil War. The area had been cleared of all vegetation so that the soldiers had a clear vision of what was coming toward them. Now the trees and underbrush clutter the trenches near the park, but the ghosts of the men marching and practicing their drills can still be seen by those like Marsha and her son who look close enough. "Taps" can still be heard by residents in the vicinity in the late afternoon.

5

FORT SMITH

The halls of Bossier City High School never rest. During the day, the student activity booms. By night, a lone confederate soldier guards the hall.

Late one evening, history teacher Miss Liz graded papers she'd assigned her class on the Civil War in Louisiana. Her concentration was broken suddenly when footsteps thudded in the corridor, then stopped abruptly in front of her classroom. She turned to see who might be outside her door. She waited, but no one knocked. She calmed her fears and reassured herself. The door was locked. The janitor knew she was there. She was safe.

She turned back to the papers, reading and marking the grades. Suddenly she halted, pen in mid-air, when the footsteps rang out again. Once more the footsteps paused before her door. "Must have been the janitor," she thought. She walked to the door and looked out. Nothing. That was enough; she decided quickly that she would not stay any longer. She'd finish grading the papers at home. As she passed through the classroom door, a cold draft made her shiver. The further down the hall she walked, the colder the air became, causing her to hurry. Her first thought was to leave, and then she thought of the janitor and started back. Halfway to the spot where he should have been, she heard screams of agony and death, and then rushed down the hall toward the exit. The janitor could take care of himself.

Miss Liz locked the main door behind her and looked back inside. A young confederate soldier stood near the door of her classroom. Judging by the look of his face, he was probably no older than some of her students. He appeared to be talking to someone. An aura of light surrounded him, lighting the entire hall. He smiled brightly as he turned to look toward her. Suddenly his attention was drawn away from her, and he

Bossier High School, where Fort Smith once stood.

snapped to attention. He saluted, and then turned away. The light surrounding him started to fade, and he vanished as he walked down the hall.

The remainder of the night, Miss Liz couldn't keep her mind on her work. She kept remembering what she had seen and wondered about the young man she had seen. Was he a ghost or was someone playing a trick on her? Some of those high school boys in her class really didn't like having to take her class. They would do anything to get back at her for the homework she had assigned. Was this one of those disgruntled students?

The next morning Miss Liz met with the janitor. She told him about the footsteps, the soldier, the cold spot, and the light surrounding him. The janitor assured her that the young soldier didn't mean her any harm. He told her he had seen the young man many times since he started to work at the school. He explained to Miss Liz that the soldier was apparently one of the men who helped guard Shreveport from attack during the Civil War.

The janitor told her he figured the young soldier had apparently been stationed at Fort Kirby Smith. He also told her that for a fifteen-year-old to join the Southern Army and be put in charge of night guard was an honor. He also told Miss Liz he'd tried to talk with the spirit but nothing ever happened. The first time the soldier started walking away down the hall and disappeared. The second time he saw the spirit, the young man saluted and left. Then late one evening, he said the soldier just stood watching as the janitor did his work. Once again, the janitor assured her there was nothing to worry about.

Miss Liz decided to stay after school the next evening. She hoped to see the ghostly figure again and wanted to try to get him to talk to her. She sat at her desk reading about the 1864 defenses and the rumored attack by General Banks. Lost deep in research, she shivered when a cold blast of air filled the room. She dropped the materials she was reading and turned in her chair.

The light from the hall told her that the nightly visitor was at her door. She reached for the knob. She thought she needed gloves on her hands as the knob was freezing to the touch. The air around her became more and more frigid. She pulled her sweater close around her shoulders. Looking into the soldier's youthful face, she recognized pride. As she lifted her hand to touch his cheek, he smiled and saluted her. She tried again to touch him, but he backed away and faded from sight. The aura around him lingered for several minutes. The temperature in the hall rose several degrees as he left. She unfolded her arms from across her stomach and stared after the ghostly light that floated down the hall.

Miss Liz returned to her desk, and there she found her papers all neatly stacked. A message was scrawled across an empty page. "I will keep learning." The soldier with the message hasn't been seen at Bossier City High School since the day Miss Liz received his message. She never saw the soldier again, but she continued to teach, hoping that the young man was there learning from her. The next semester, she taught her students about the fortifications that surrounded Shreveport and why they were so important to the Civil War.

Fort Smith was one of the major fortifications in the line of defense the Confederates held during the early part of the Civil War. By controlling the forts around Shreveport, the Confederates controlled the Red River, one of the main waterways in Louisiana. The Union Navy felt they had to clean up this major waterway still in Confederate hands and take control of it. It was one of three thrusts planned by General Grant in 1864. A successful campaign to take the major waterway was meant to cripple the Confederates. Their Trans-Mississippi position was a threat to the Union Army. The Yanks planned to destroy the supplies and industry of the South. They figured their army would defeat the Rebels at the forts surrounding Shreveport. All would be lost for the Confederates if these fortifications failed.

General Banks wanted to impress President Lincoln. Banks felt Grant was the only general who was getting any recognition, and he wanted his part of the glory. Banks intended to capture the huge store of cotton in Western Louisiana, thereby saving the U. S. Treasury upward of $100 million. He hoped to be the one to defeat the Confederate Army by cutting off supplies and taking the cotton, the major industry of the South. Banks asked permission to carry out his ideas in the Trans-Mississippi area.

General Grant thought he would put Banks to the test. He was dubious about the man's abilities. He told Banks to put the squeeze on the Rebel headquarters at Shreveport. Grant wanted Banks to secure other major southern posts as well. However, the fighting never reached the battery or the forts around Shreveport. No shots of war were ever fired at Fort Kirby Smith or any of the other Shreveport fortifications.

Fort Kirby Smith was constructed much the same as the other forts in the area, by slave labor as well as the labor of citizens and soldiers. Trenches were dug and mounds of dirt were piled up to build earthen walls. The brush was cleared away so soldiers had a clear view of the river and the land surrounding Shreveport.

The soldiers were made up of men from the Shreveport area. Some were old, and some were young. Some were very young and fresh out of school. Some should have still been in school. Ben was only fifteen, but he wanted to serve his country and run the Yankees out of the South. What he really wanted was to fight alongside Jefferson Davis, but that was not possible, so he joined the nearest regiment, much to his parents' disappointment. They wanted him to stay in school and make something of himself. Ben wouldn't listen.

Late one night, Ben drew guard duty, and he was proud that the sergeant had chosen him for this most important duty. He marched up and down where he was told. His footsteps were soft in the mounded dirt of the fortress walls. He hoped he would encounter an enemy so he could further impress his commanding officer. However, Ben was never to meet with an enemy soldier. The first and last night of his guard duty, Ben was killed—

not by an enemy, but by his own clumsiness. In the dark, Ben wasn't watching where he was walking very well. He stumbled and fell on his own rifle bayonet. He was found dead the next morning.

A monument attesting to the fact that Fort Kirby Smith existed stands at Coleman Street between Monroe and Mansfield Streets. The walking park where Fort Smith once stood is to the side and a little in front of Bossier High School. It is a serene place to meditate. The trenches and the breastworks of the old fort are no longer visible in the park or the surrounding area. Bossier High School was built on top of most of Fort Smith. Although there was no fighting at the fort, one soldier, Ben, took his guard duty seriously enough to remain on as guard. He may still roam the halls of the school at night trying to learn what he can. He may even be seen at the walking park.

The Fort Smith monument, commemorating the fort and its namesake, General Kirby E. Smith.

II

Crossroads Country

The Post at Opelousas

Poste du Rapides

Los Adaes

Camp Salubrity

Fort Beauregard

Fort Buhlow

Fort Charles/Beaufort

Fort Jesup

Fort Randolph

Fort St. Jean Baptiste

Fort Selden

Fort of the Natchez

6

THE POST AT OPELOUSAS

The Post at Opelousas was actually established in 1720, making it the third oldest city in the state. The post was possibly built on top of the burial mounds of the Native American tribe, the Attakapas. Opelousas means "black leg." The Indians painted their legs black to contrast with the light color of their bodies.

Hank, a young man who lived near Opelousas, used to walk the hills in the area. As a child, he searched those hills for arrowheads, especially after the rains came. He loved for the rain to fall and wash away the dirt that hid the precious collectibles. He often found pieces he kept to complete several of his collections. If he didn't need them, he tossed them back into the hills. Hank had no idea he was walking and playing on burial mounds that were over twelve thousand years old. But he read all he could about the Attakapas Indians.

Late one evening, Hank roamed the hills, kicking at the loosened dirt and dragging a stick behind him. As he walked, he felt a freezing cold draft blowing in from the treetops, even though it was the middle of summer. A fog quickly started oozing out of the ground. Inch by inch, the fog enveloped him from his feet to his head. It was as if someone pulled a foggy curtain over and around him. The next thing that happened frightened him so badly he couldn't move. He felt as if his feet were stuck in mud and muck. He couldn't lift his feet or move them at all. His legs were too heavy to lift. He heard loud chanting voices coming out of the fog. Hank shivered at the eerie sounds and wanted to run, but he stayed; he had no choice. He felt as if he were paralyzed. There were unrecognizable voices shouting in the fog. He began to feel really cold. His summer shirt did little to keep out the dampness of the fog or the cold air. More alarming than the cold, though, the chanting and noise grew louder and louder. The longer he stood on the hills, the colder he became.

Suddenly, he saw forms coming toward him through the fog. The filmy forms moved slowly at first, with no real direction. Closer and closer the forms came as they began to take shape into men and women. Finally several men danced around him while the women knelt in the background.

Hank watched, more frightened than ever, as some of the men danced closer. The other dancers stopped and faded away for a few minutes. Minutes later, they returned with a limp and lifeless body. They laid the body on the ground, then wrapped it in furs and then left it on the ground in front of him. The men faded into nothingness and the women began chanting in low moaning voices. The singing grew louder as the shapes in the fog became more and more frantic. They reappeared in the full glory of dance as before.

Abruptly, the dancing stopped, and one of the spirit men stepped forward. There were more shouts in words he did not understand. An Indian man shouted and pointed to Hank and then to the fur-wrapped body at his feet. Hank still didn't understand what they were saying, but he knew the spirits were burying one of their own. He felt as if the man wanted him to look at the body. As he reached down to the furs, he drew back quickly. He didn't want to look. He'd been to one funeral, but this was not the same thing. He had read about Indian burials when he went to the library.

Frightened, Hank stood still and watched. He listened. The one spirit that stood over the body shook some sort of powder over the dead person. He mumbled and then cried out loud. Hank was startled when the girls and women started crying again. For a long time the man cried. The women fell to their knees, bowing and chanting. Finally they stood and turned their backs on the body and faded away into the fog. After several minutes, the dancers withdrew, and the fog lifted slowly. Hank reached down quickly, and flipped back the fur, and stared into a face that was identical to his. Then the body disappeared. He was able to feel his feet again. As the fog lifted, he left, hastily.

As a grown man, he continues to return to the hills where he searches the mounds for artifacts and for the spirits. He still wonders about the body in the furs. On occasion he is still confronted with the black-legged Native American spirits. Their light-colored bodies dance frantically in the curtain of fog, but he never has figured out whom the natives are burying because the furs are empty.

The French arrived in Opelousas around 1690 as explorers, hunters, and trappers. Opelousas began as a trading post. The men who first settled the area traded with each other and with the Opelousas Indians. The French often took wives from among the Indians.

Once the settlers came to the Opelousas area, they applied for and were granted lands. Some of these men stayed and raised families with their

Indian wives, while others stayed only a while and moved on to other areas of Louisiana. In 1720, Opelousas was officially established, making it the third largest city in the state and the third oldest. Louis Pellerin attained a land grant in 1782 and laid out the town. Soon the Spanish took control of Opelousas, and it became a military post. The carefully kept records of the French and the Spanish provide historical information about the people who lived in the area at the time. A list dated June 8, 1777, contains the names of ten officers of the Opelousas Post Militia and its ninety-nine Fusiliers who served as protectors of the Old Spanish Fort, better known as the Post at Opelousas.

Sketch of the Old Spanish Fort. Sketch by J. A. Allen.

In 1803, the United States acquired a large portion of land, the Louisiana Purchase, doubling its area. The Post at Opelousas was part of it. It remained a military post until Opelousas was incorporated in 1821. At that time, there were only forty-seven soldiers at the post.

One of the forty-seven soldiers, a man named Hawkins, was married to a beautiful Attakapas Indian maiden. They were married according to the tribal customs. The couple lived in the Opelousas area outside the fort walls and raised several children until the soldier's untimely death, shortly after his sixth child was born. The army was going to bury Hawkins in the post cemetery, but his wife's family came in the night and stole his body. Hawkins was buried according to the Attakapas tribal tradition at the ceremonial mounds that held the bones of all their ancestors.

In 1862, Camp Opelousas became a Confederate camp where soldiers were instructed. Colonel Marigny commanded the soldiers. After the fall of Baton Rouge to the Union, Opelousas became the capital of Louisiana for a short time.

After the Civil War came the reconstruction of the South. U. S. troops were often sent to the Post of Opelousas. In November of 1867, Captain W.

Opelousas was the capital of Louisiana for a while during the Civil War. This is the governor's mansion. Sketch by J. A. Allen.

W. Webb and his 4th U. S. Cavalry of ninety men manned the post. Two years later, records show that Company H, 15th Infantry was commanded at Opelousas by Captain Frank M. Coke.

To visit Opelousas, drive down Interstate 49 to exit 15–19 at the junction of U. S. Highway 190 and you will be in Opelousas, the original site of the third oldest city in the state.

The fort has been swallowed up by a growing city. There is a historical marker and nothing more of the old Post at Opelousas, unless of course visitors want to count the dancing Attakapas Indians, who resent anyone snooping around their eternal burial grounds.

7

POSTE DU RAPIDES

Poste du Rapides was constructed halfway down the road to the entrance to the Red River and Natchitoches. Near the grand rapids of the Red River is the place where Helen walks to clear her head and sort out her troubles from time to time. The first time she walked along the river banks, she became acquainted with a headless specter. She felt as if she were being followed and kept looking back over her shoulder. Every once in a while she would stop and, turning slowly, she would see nothing.

When she came to her private place and sat upon a large rock to peer out across the rapids, she once again felt a presence nearby. She looked around to see if she could spot anything out of the ordinary. The next thing she knew, something appeared in front of her, something she'd never seen before. The ghost of a man came from out of the woods carrying a head under its arm. The head had a huge gash of opened skin that oozed fresh blood. The hair had been scalped from the top of the head. The light, ghostly form floated across the earth and rocks to where she sat.

The specter stalked menacingly closer to Helen. It circled the rock where she sat. Helen sat up, ready to run but waiting. Then she eased down from her perch and slowly started toward her vehicle. She looked back, and the spirit vanished back into the woods. Stopping short, Helen waited a few minutes and walked back to the rock. Again the specter came out of the woods toward her with the head still tucked under its arm. She watched the expression on the face change from intimidation to terror. A blood-curdling scream blurted from the mouth of the head. Helen wanted to run away but instead spoke softly. She tried to convey to the ghostly image that she was not there to disturb it or the area. The spirit seemed to understand. After circling her a few times, the wispy form went back into the woods, dissolving into a vapor as it disappeared.

Each time Helen goes out to the rapids, the specter greets her, and she tells it the same thing. She doesn't want to hurt anything there. The specter always fades back into the woods. Helen loves the peace and quiet at the rapids. However, in the past it wasn't always so peaceful.

In 1722, Inspector General Sieur Diron d'Artaguette wrote a report to his superiors about a Frenchman at the Poste de Rapids settlement. The man and two daughters were drying their clothing when attacked by Chickasaw Indians. The daughters were taken prisoners by the Indians and were never seen again. The Frenchman was not nearly as fortunate. He was captured and beheaded. The captors scalped him and took the scalp with them. His body and head were left to the wild animals and other scavengers in the woods. The three Natchitoches Indians who were with the man and his daughters escaped injury by hiding in the woods.

There is no official documentation to confirm the existence of a Poste de Rapides. However, many historians believe that in 1723, the site was established in central Louisiana.

Sieur Diron d'Artaguette came up the Red River and reported to his superiors. He wrote about many varieties of fish that were plentiful. He told of the Red River, navigable for only seven to eight months of the year up to the rapids. The inspector maintained that a post on "le grand rapide" near Fort St. Jean Baptiste was needed. This is the point on the river where it became impassable. He described the beheading of a Frenchman and the capture of the man's two daughters when they were attacked by the Chickasaw Indians.

Governor Bienville knew it was important for the settlers to have protection, and he recommended to his superiors that the fort be built. This post was critical to the French keeping their hold on the land up to the Red River. The Spanish considered the land up to the Red River from Texas as their territory. This was the main reason the post at Natchitoches was established by Louis Antoine Juchereau de St. Denis.

St. Denis was commandant of Fort St. Jean Baptiste. He also saw a need for another fort in the Natchitoches area. The Poste du Rapides was dependent on the older Natchitoches fort for a time. Some of the French soldiers who manned the post decided to stay. They settled the wilderness near the Red River at the Grand Rapids.

In 1767, Chevalier de Villiers wrote to his superiors of being given assistance by Monsieur Layssard at the Post du Rapides. Later in 1770, Layssard was appointed commandant of the Rapids District. Governor O'Reilly wanted to free the area of "disreputable people, deserters and evil traders." He wanted to prevent smuggling and therefore gave Layssard strict instructions about mule trains traveling across the land.

After the revolutionary threats and actions of French colonists, the governor ordered a survey of the people in the rapids area. The reports made by Eduardo Nugent and Juan Kelly showed thirty-three whites and eighteen slaves. They reported eight houses belonging to eight poor inhabitants. The residents of the settlement raised tobacco and corn and had a few cows to keep them in food. The report also included information about a small band of Apalache Indians.

Commandants of the Poste du Rapides included Etienne and Valentine Layssard, Joseph Chevalier, Poiret, Caesar Archinard, Jean Archinard, and Ennemond Muellion. Their duties were simply to keep the peace. They acted as do modern-day justices of the peace.

Les Rapides was the name that stuck for the area because of the rapids of the Red River. The political developments taking place far away in Washington, New Orleans, France, and Spain increased interest in the Port at New Orleans. The settlers at the Post de Rapides had no idea about the changes that were forthcoming for them or the world around them.

The Poste du Rapides was located somewhere near the beginning of the rapids on the Red River not far from Fort St. Jean Baptiste. There is nothing left of the fort except court depositions of men who were apparently commanders of the fortress. Of course, the legend and the spirit of the headless Frenchman is another reason for believing that the Poste du Rapides existed in the late 1790s.

8

LOS ADAES

Out of Natchitoches about thirty miles, Los Adaes lies quietly waiting for visitors to take advantage of what the historical site has to offer. Danny, the reenactor, stands at the top of the stairs, smiling. With the background of woods behind him, he looks like a French settler from the past. His white pants and shirt and moccasined feet are period costumes in which he feels at ease, most of the time.

Danny doesn't just watch for tourists who want to know the history of Los Adaes. He also keeps an eye out for a white dog known to roam the woods surrounding the site. Although it has been seen by several visitors to the fort, Danny has yet to see the elusive animal. He says if the dog is around it is closely followed by the ghost of a French woman who was tortured and killed in front of the fort.

A large white dog sometimes greets the tourists after Danny leaves them to explore the Los Adaes site. Other times it is a small white dog. Others have said it is a white puppy. Sharon, a woman who visited the site, said she was met at her vehicle by a nosy pup. She was afraid at first but remembered that any time a dog smells you and wags its tail, it is friendly. She had always been fond of animals anyway, and she thought it must belong to someone who lived in the vicinity. The woman looked around but saw no houses and didn't recall passing any on her way to the fort.

Reaching down, she patted the dog on the head and walked up the steps to the small museum building at the Los Adaes State Park. There, she expressed her thought about the white dog to Danny. He hurried to the door to get a glimpse of the white dog. Nothing was outside the door. He told her there was no dog in the area of that particular description, but he had heard that, if a white dog is around, there must be a ghost there too. Sharon stepped back outside to see if the dog was still where she left it when she came inside. Nothing could be found—no trace of the pup, nothing. Danny followed her outside. They came back into the museum, and he gave her the tour, telling her the story of the Indian attack and the kidnapped woman. Afterward, she chose to walk the grounds alone.

As Sharon strolled around the outline of the palisades, she heard a faint whimper behind her. She turned, to be licked on the hand, this time by a large white dog. She patted his head and continued on her way, remembering what Danny had told her. At the front gates area of the fortress, she noticed the dog had not stayed with her. She saw it at the edge of the woods. Sharon started in the direction of the dog but thought better of it for a moment.

Turning away slightly, out of the corner of her eye, she saw the dog disappear into the woods. Bewildered at the mysterious disappearance of the beautiful dog, she turned back to the outline of the fort, intent on the historical site. She stepped across one of the timbers outlining the fort and nearly bumped into another woman walking the grounds. The woman jumped back and stumbled away from Sharon. The period costume the woman wore made Sharon think she must be part of the reenactment team the state park provided as entertainment for the visitors. Sharon's background in costuming made her sure that the woman was representative of the French middle class. Sharon stopped abruptly. She took stock of the woman's disheveled appearance. Her clothing was filthy. On closer inspection of the woman's clothes, Sharon noticed they were tattered and torn. Dried blood covered her arms and face. Her hair was a tangled mass of caked blood and dirt. Rawhide tethers dangled from the woman's wrists. Sharon watched the woman closely and saw her nearly trip over the tethers tied about her ankles. Sharon went after the woman and approached her to try to help. The closer she came, the louder the woman cried and moaned. Sharon reached out her hand to the poor woman. Before she could touch her, the woman disappeared in a wisp of cold air, her eyes staring hollowly at Sharon.

Sharon hurried away from where she'd seen the woman and nearly tripped over the white dog, which waited at her feet for only a moment and then bounded away into thin air. At that point Sharon remembered what she had heard on television and what Danny had told her: "Sometimes white dogs appear just before a ghostly spirit appears." Sharon knew the woman she'd seen was a ghost. She was the ghost of the kidnapped woman that the Indians had killed in front of Los Adaes.

Once considered the capital of Texas, Los Adaes is one of the most intriguing forts in Louisiana. It was the scene of unique cooperation between French and Spanish soldiers and settlers and the Native Americans of the area. Los Adaes was built to keep the French rulers from overrunning the Texas territory.

Water well at Los Adaes.

Los Adaes was surrounded by a hexagonal stockade incorporating three bulwarks. Inside the walls were several buildings. These included a chapel, a guardhouse, barracks, water wells, a powder house, and a blacksmith shop. The governor had his residence built inside the walls of Los Adaes, where it remained for forty-four years.

A French woman was taken hostage by the Natchez Indians because of the killing done by the Frenchmen. The Indians had attacked the settlers of Los Adaes, and the settlers ran down the raiders. When they caught up with the men who had attacked the fortress, the Frenchmen hanged the Indians. The bodies of those killed were left where they died.

Enraged at the diabolical event, the Natchez Indians retaliated. A middle-class French woman was taken from her home in Natchitoches. She was badly abused by the natives before they brought her to Los Adaes. Once at the fort, the Natchez Indians, using the poor woman as a shield, staked her spread-eagled in front of one of the bulwarks where she could be seen by the men inside the walls of the fortress.

The woman's screams of terror and moans of pain were heard by all. The soldiers listened to the natives screaming for blood—"Sang-sang!" The torture lasted for three days before she was finally killed. The natives left her mutilated body staked to the ground and faded into the woods. She was buried nearby by the soldiers.

Life for the one hundred soldiers posted at Los Adaes was very harsh. Their families' homes were built outside the walls of the fortress along with the army's corrals, service buildings, and the homes of the Indians. Soldiers at Los Adaes were mostly Mexican cavalrymen sent to defend the San Miguel Mission. They also escorted the governor and missionaries on their travels through the province. The nearest Spanish suppliers for the Mexicans were some eight hundred miles away, so they traded with the French and Native Americans in Natchitoches.

The soldiers and their families would otherwise have perished from starvation. Their supplies were often spoiled from too much rain. The land was poor, and the crops failed more often than not. Constant food shortages prompted the illicit trade with the French. The Mexicans disobeyed orders not to trade with the enemy, and even the governor at Los Adaes participated in this trade process. The commercial trade was a big boost to the settlers in the settlement of Natchitoches. It suffered a severe recession when Los Adaes was closed in 1773.

The Mexican troops packed up and left Los Adaes and made the trek to San Antonio. After the war between Texas and Mexico, the soldiers who had served at Los Adaes scattered. Some went west or south, but many returned to the Natchitoches area to settle.

Los Adaes lies just off the road at 6354 Highway 485, and is one mile northeast of Robeline. The fort site lies between Fort Jesup of the Confederate States of America (CSA) and Fort St. Jean Baptiste CSA. To reach the fourteen-acre site from Interstate 49, exit onto Louisiana State Highway 6 west. Turn west onto State Highway 485 and follow the signs. At the fort site, visitors can find a headquarters building and a small museum of artifacts. There is a walking tour of the fort site that takes about forty-five minutes to an hour. There are timbers marking the outline of the presidio. The trail is marked with numbered and arrowed rocks showing where well pits and thatched jacales once stood. If visitors are lucky, they may see the ghost of the lady who was murdered in front of the Los Adaes fort gates. She appears before some of the visitors while the white dog greets others and takes them on the tour of the fort.

9

CAMP SALUBRITY

Not well known in the area, Camp Salubrity is about twenty-five miles from Fort Jesup, which is also called Camp Salubrity at times. In the piney woods up on a high ridge, the spirit of a soldier from the Texas-Mexican War stands his post. On this ridge, there are no mosquitoes or other insects. The spirit of the first soldier to lose his life at Camp Salubrity keeps all away. Even dogs dare not go up on the ridge where Camp Salubrity once stood.

In his memoirs, Ulysses S. Grant says, "The first death at Camp Salubrity was an accident." Walking guard, a young soldier continues to take care of his duty around Camp Salubrity's perimeter just as he did before his untimely death. His spirit has been seen by many, but one man in particular tells his story abut Camp Salubrity.

As a young man, Charlie enjoyed taking his hound dogs up on the ridge where Camp Salubrity once stood. He first saw the spirit of the young soldier at night. Charlie's hounds had gotten on the trail of something right away. He followed them for a while and decided they were just running in circles on top of the mountain. He made a fire and sat and listened to the beautiful voices of his hounds. Maggie's low rumbling bawl as she sniffed out the game and Rusty's immature soprano bark resounded off the surrounding hills. They were on the trail of something.

As Charlie sat listening to the opera of the chase, at first he didn't see the strange misty figure walking out of the woods. Once he saw the figure, he was a little frightened, but he knew he could outrun anything if he had to. He looked closely at the ghostly figure, noting that there was dried blood on the man's face. Charlie knew the man needed help. Charlie was known to be the friendliest man in town, and he proved it once again. He invited the strange man to sit at the campfire. The soldier ignored the offer. This perturbed Charlie. He expected to be treated as he tried to treat others. He approached the spirit soldier, but the man sidestepped Charlie and stumbled off into the woods. Charlie went into the woods and brush after the man. He searched for hours but could not find him.

When Charlie got back to the fire, he settled back to listen to the dogs again. However, there was no barking from either dog. He sat up quickly and cocked his head to the side. There was nothing. No sounds. Nothing. Suddenly he heard a yip from Rusty and then another from Maggie. A few minutes later, both dogs came running with their tails tucked between their legs. This strange behavior puzzled Charlie greatly. These were his two best dogs. They didn't shy away from anything.

Both dogs cowered at Charlie's feet like whipped pups. He couldn't figure out what was going on until, out of the woods, the spirit of the soldier entered the circle of campfire light. The dogs whimpered and ducked behind Charlie's legs. The ghostly spirit moved toward Charlie and his dogs. As the spirit stepped into the fire, sparks flew in all directions into the damp night air. Charlie shivered in the frigid aftermath of the spirit passing through his fire. The dogs let out low guttural growls as the spirit passed. The hair on the dogs' backs stood on end. Charlie rubbed his arms where goose bumps had popped up on his skin.

Charlie took his dogs to the mountain only one other time since that first night. The hounds milled around, sniffing the ground, then the air, before they ran off into the night searching for game. The dogs never sniffed the trail of another animal that night. All the wildlife and birds seemed to be in hiding. Charlie waited for a while. He shivered uncontrollably. He didn't really know why until he felt a strange coldness envelope the area. Then he knew why he'd returned. He wanted to make sure he'd seen what he thought he had the last trip out. Within moments of the cold draft, the bloody soldier stumbled toward him. Charlie looked into the man's death-riddled eyes.

"What happened to you?" Charlie asked the spirit. No answer was given. The spirit soldier stopped and stood in front of Charlie. Once more Charlie approached and asked the specter what had happened. The soldier stared at Charlie, and then turned to walk away. Charlie reached out and touched the sleeve of the boy's uniform but came back with nothing but a handful of air. The spirit stumbled toward the woods. "Wait." Charlie cried. "Who are you? What happened?" The soldier turned back and smiled at Charlie for a few moments, then vanished into the woods.

Charlie no longer hunts the property where Camp Salubrity once stood. The fort sits on private property now, and there is no hunting on the piney ridge for anyone.

In the Piney Woods of Louisiana between the Red River and the Sabine lies the property on which Camp Salubrity once lay. The camp was set up about three miles from Natchitoches and three miles before coming to Grand Ecore. The camp was on high ground, away from the river. Its name fit it perfectly. The camp was very good for the soldiers' health, with no mosquitoes to cause malaria or other diseases. The mosquitoes were not on the high ridge as they were down in the valley. The swarms of infection-carrying insects made life miserable for others, but the high ground protected the soldiers. The climate at the camp was most favorable for the soldiers as well. The ground under Camp Salubrity was sandy and high on a pine ridge. The water from the springs was pure and cool.

Camp Salubrity was occupied by the 3rd Infantry of the Union Army during a six-month period. In May of 1844, Ulysses S. Grant came to the camp before he went off to fight in the Texas–Mexican War and finally become general and then president. The 4th Infantry came to Camp Salubrity in May of 1844 as well. They had instructions to occupy the camp and wait for further orders. In the beginning, officers and enlisted men alike used canvas tents, but as the air heated, the tents were covered with sheds. These sheds helped to break the heat. These were the only buildings to resemble permanency until much later in the winter months. Visiting with the planters along the river and Fort Jesup, twenty-five miles away, helped the soldiers live through a hot, boring summer.

As summer days became shorter and cooler, the nights grew colder, and the shaded tents obviously afforded little comfort for the men stationed at the camp. The expected duty orders still didn't come. The soldiers were put to work, cutting timbers to build much needed and more permanent lodgings. The huts were healthier housing than the tents and were built for officers and enlisted soldiers alike. The winter ended up being much more agreeable than the summer. The men occasionally attended parties along the bottom land on the Red River hosted by the planters in the area, especially during the holiday season. About this time, the first death of Camp Salubrity occurred. It was purely an accident. One of the young soldiers had wandered out into the woods to do some hunting early one morning. Some of the men were just awakening and some were milling about, getting ready to have breakfast. Two shots rang out and a voice shouted for help. Several of the men ran toward the voice. By the time they reached the soldier, he was almost dead. He had shot at a flock of turkeys. He shot the second time, but the rifle had exploded in his face. The soldier's face was bloodied and torn apart. The shell had also torn through his upper chest, making him the camp's first casualty.

Not until July 1845 were "further orders" sent to the men at Camp Salubrity. The infantry was ordered to move to New Orleans Barracks. This left Camp Salubrity empty for a time. It was sporadically manned until the Civil War began. In late April 1865, a Confederate brigade of men on the march came to the camp. This brigade lost thirty-eight men during the war, either killed or mortally wounded. Sixty-nine men died of disease.

The brigade stayed until May 19, 1865, when they were dismissed from service. The men were told to go home, as the surrender of the Trans-Mississippi Department was anticipated.

Camp Salubrity was located approximately two to three miles from Natchitoches to the northwest. The Camp Salubrity site is on private property off State Highway 1. Markings of the huts' foundations can be seen only with great effort. Nothing else of the fort exists today—nothing but the one soldier whose death was just an accident, and who remains on guard.

10

FORT BEAUREGARD

Day fades into dusk in Catahoula Parish on the Ouachita River, and darkness fades into weird, unearthly transformations. The hill where Fort Beauregard once stood becomes enveloped in a pervasive darkness. Eerie shapes of gray mist form in the night, floating here and there. As the shapes wander above the earth lightly, they moan and shriek in pain.

Several young men from Harrisonburg heard from a few of their friends about strange things happening out at the old fort site. Four boys, fortified with their favorite brew, decided to check out the action at the fort. They sat on the tailgate of their truck with their lights on. They waited for the macabre scene they had been told about. Their wait was short-lived. As they sat on the truck, scenes from hell surrounded them slowly and methodically. In slow motion, the area filled with the spirits of battle-torn soldiers.

Men with tattered, bloody clothes and mangled limbs walked toward the truck lights. Some of the spirits had no way of seeing, as they had their faces blown away. Others limped, flaying the air with stubs for arms. Then gaunt twisted faces filled the air with screams of terror. The night wore on in a confusing dance of death. Horses and mules lay slaughtered and dying. Some of the animals still kicked in pain. The spirits of the dead reached up to the boys, trying to grab their clothes. One young man nearly lost his boots to a barefoot soldier. Cries of pain and death filled the air. The specters even tried to climb on the truck with the boys. For what seemed like hours, the boys watched the horrible scene unfold. They were unable to move and get away.

The smell of blood, decay, and death surrounded the boys. Battlefield violence and carnage were evident everywhere. Shells were lobbed from the darkness in the vicinity of the river and came straight at their truck. Fire belched from the cannons on board ironclad ships on the water. The young men decided that evacuation was the best action to take. They tore themselves

Animals were expendable in wartime. Photo courtesy of the Opelousas Chamber of Commerce.

from their paralyzed positions and sped off into the night. After they left the perimeter of Fort Beauregard, they turned back for a final look. There was nothing but the tracks left by the truck. The carnage and violence, the spirits and dead animals, were all gone.

The high school boys who saw the Fort Beauregard action never returned to the site. At times in the past, high school boys had used the fort as an initiation tradition, but no longer. The episodes at the fort became more terrifying each time someone visited it after dark. The boys recommend that no one disturb the specters at Fort Beauregard.

Confederates built Fort Beauregard behind Harrisonburg on the Ouachita River to help protect Monroe. Federal gunboats threatened to come upriver to attack. Union Commodore C. E. Woodworth brought a flotilla of four gunboats as far as Fort Beauregard and opened fire on the Confederates. With only two cannons in the fort, the Southern soldiers fought back. The gunboats withdrew, only to return the next day. For approximately an hour and a half, the gunboats again fired on the fort.

Part of the Crescent Regiment under the leadership of Lieutenant Colonel George W. Logan, the 15th Louisiana Cavalry under the command of Major Isaac F. Harrison, and a group of artillerymen under Captain Thomas Benton held off the Union invasion. Besides damage to the fort, both sides suffered casualties, and the wounded were many. The carnage after the battle at Fort Beauregard was ghastly. Soldiers' faces were blown away; their bodies were ripped apart from the shelling of the ironclad ships. The Confederates held their ground despite the one hundred and twenty shells fired by the Union gunboats. The wounded were mostly beyond help and died at the fort in the hands of the Union Army or were sent to prison camps with others who were captured. Those who were lucky enough to get away and fight another time were left with minor wounds, and their clothing was in bad need of replacing. Some of the men didn't have shoes to wear as theirs had worn out and there was no way to replace them.

In September 1863, Colonel Logan and about forty soldiers evacuated Fort Beauregard. The Confederate soldiers added to the damage of the Union shells and destroyed the magazine. They set fire to the fort as they were leaving. The Federal soldiers spiked all but two guns left by the Rebels. They hauled off the two remaining small cannons when they too left Fort Beauregard.

On a hill behind the small community of Harrisburg in the Catahoula Parish is the site where the historical Fort Beauregard once stood off of State Highway 124. Nothing is left of Fort Beauregard except the foundations of the casements of the earthen fort and perhaps the spirits of several soldiers who still defend the fort on the Ouachita River.

11

FORT BUHLOW

Standing on the ground once occupied by Fort Buhlow, Buck rubbed his eyes. He couldn't believe what he saw. Fog rolled in across the Red River a bit thicker than usual for that time of year. A ship drifted through the mist, headed up river. It was hard to see with the fog so dense, but as it steamed closer to the fort, Buck could see the image of an ironclad ship.

Buck watched the ironclad ship, which looked a lot like the pictures he had seen of the *CSS Missouri*, take shape out of the mist and drift past the earthen works of Fort Buhlow on its way upstream. The outline of the ship disappeared eerily up the river. Water droplets shone on the paddle-wheel as the moon peeped through the fog occasionally. Quietly, the heavy ship slipped through the water. The paddles dipped into the water, bringing it up and spilling it over as it went to take another bite of water. The rushing water from the paddles should have made churning noises. The water foamed as the wheels rotated and plowed through, but there was no noise. No sounds from the pent-up steam screaming through the gauge-cocks were ever heard. The throbbing of the engine could not be heard. For what seemed like hours, the ship floated back and forth, up and down the river.

Buck couldn't stop watching the apparition. He felt as if time had stood still, and he thought it was late when he left the river to return home. Back in his vehicle, however, he discovered he had been at the river for only a few minutes.

After a couple of nights, he brought a buddy out to the point where he'd seen the ship. The same thing happened again. A heavy mist shrouded the area, and the *CSS Missouri* made its appearance shortly after the fog covered them. His buddy had teased Buck mercilessly when he told him about the ghost ship. When the friend saw the ship for himself, he apologized to Buck. The ship made several runs back and forth on the water. Neither man heard the engines or the paddlewheels hit the water. The droplets glistened in the moonlight, and the water frothed as the wheel bit through the depth of the river. Buck's friend went home and refused to come back to fish with Buck again.

Later, Buck and his wife came to the river, and they both saw the *CSS Missouri* make its nightly run up and down the river. That night they saw a soldier walking around in the pilothouse of the ghost ship. They couldn't really tell much about him other than that he was carrying a gun on his shoulder.

Buck also claims that the fishing in the river is never any good when the ghostly ship is on the water. Sometimes, he says, he can tell when the ship is going to be on the water because of the lack of fish biting. Both Buck and his wife felt as if they were there for hours instead of just minutes.

The *CSS Missouri* ironclad made several runs a week guarding the river from Union attack. There were usually a couple of soldiers on deck to spot other gunboats that might be on the river as well. Often the soldiers at Fort Buhlow could see the soldiers in the wheelhouse of the ironclad and would wave at them. The soldiers on the boats always waved back. The *CSS Missouri* and Fort Buhlow never saw combat, nor did many of the other forts on the Red River. The ironclad ship *CSS Missouri* was surrendered in Alexandria on June 3, 1865.

On the Pineville side of the Red River are the remains of the Fort Buhlow breastworks along Lake Buhlow. Because of an anticipated attack by Union soldiers under the guidance of General Nathaniel Banks, Fort Buhlow and two other forts were planned. One of those, to be the largest of the three, was never finished, but Fort Buhlow was finished by March 1865. The work had been done by fifteen hundred soldiers and many civilians. Approximately five hundred slaves were forced to dig the earthen trenches and pile up the breastwork mounds, working much longer hours than the others. Construction began on the earthworks in October of 1864. A military engineer, Lieutenant A. Buhlow, designed and supervised the construction of the fort named after him.

Fort Buhlow was built on a promontory overlooking the Red River. It was a roughly circular type of earthen fortification consisting of trenches and mounds of earth surrounded by a moat, much like many other forts of the era. The earthen walls were thirty feet high and two hundred feet in diameter. The vegetation in and around the fort had to be cleared in order for the soldiers to have a clear view of what might be coming toward them. The military authorities were able to provide the soldiers with only twelve cannons for their protection. The ironclad ship *CSS Missouri* made regular runs up and down the river as further protection was needed for the fort.

The buildup of the Confederate troops in Alexandria and the fact that the ironclad ship *CSS Missouri* was docked on the Red River opposite Fort Buhlow at Fort Randolph only six hundred yards downstream apparently helped to hold off the much anticipated Union attack by General Banks. No fighting ever took place at Fort Buhlow.

When a roadside park was built east of the fort, most of the breastworks had to be cleared for parking and recreation. This caused damage to the earthwork trenches. Fort Buhlow has little of its origins left, but visitors can discern where the fort was located.

In 1928, several patriotic societies saw that historical markers were placed at the site of the fort. The markers were constructed with the bricks taken from the old Louisiana Seminary buildings. After reading the site marker for Fort Buhlow, visitors can walk around on the earthworks, then go down into the trenches where soldiers waited for attack, feel the tension of the state's history.

Fort Buhlow was located near Alexandria on the east side of the Red River. The fort site is on the north side of U.S. Highway 71, only six hundred yards from Fort Randolph on the south side of the same highway.

The marker and some of the trenches are all that is left of Fort Buhlow except the spirit of the *CSS Missouri* and its men. They too are a part of the state's history. Visitors who look closely enough and are at the fort at the right time of day may be able to catch a glimpse of the large ghostly ironclad ship and the men who run it as it floats by the fort site.

Buck believes the ironclad ship is still on patrol laying mines in the river for enemy ships.

12

FORT CHARLES/BEAUFORT

Beaufort Plantation, once a bed-and-breakfast, sits atop the place where Fort Charles once stood. The gracious old home welcomed tourists and travelers who came to enjoy the Southern hospitality that dates to the 1700s, when Fort Charles was first established.

One couple, Chas and Jane, called for reservations and were given their confirmation number for their selected dates. They drove to Beaufort through a beautiful lane overlapped by strong, tall live oaks. Upon arrival, they were greeted in much the same fashion as visitors would have been in the antebellum South. The couple was amazed at how welcomed they felt and how quickly they were greeted. The manager settled them for the night and told them she'd have their breakfast ready early the next morning. As soon as the manager left them alone for the night, Jane put away their things, and they began to get ready for bed.

Jane lit the candles on the night stand. A slight breeze blew through the room and immediately the flames went out. She tried again, and once more, the breeze blew out the candles. Chas tried to find the source of the extra air, but he found no doors or windows open to allow the wind inside. Finally they gave up and went to bed.

They had been asleep for only a few minutes when they heard noises from downstairs. At first they thought they heard doors opening and closing and sometimes slamming. Chas got out of bed and went downstairs to see if anyone else was in the house. The doors were all locked, and nothing was out of place. Back in bed, the couple drifted off to sleep again. An hour or so later, they were awakened by sounds of arguing and doors slamming again. When they went to investigate, Jane noticed the freezing cold temperature in the room. She pulled her wrapper closer and followed Chas. They still found nothing. The entire night went much the same. Jane mumbled to Chas about his cold feet when she felt someone crawling into the bed. When he sat up and asked her what she was talking about, she squealed and jumped from the bed. Confused, Chas followed her. They watched as the covers on the bed were slowly pulled up and a lump formed underneath. They yanked the sheets and blanket back to reveal nothing. Chase slept in the chair and Jane on the settee in the room.

At the break of dawn, the smell of breakfast floated up the stairs. As they rose for the day, they discussed the happenings of the night before. They shrugged it all off to active imaginations and started downstairs for their breakfast. Both had marveled over the beautiful antiques in the house the night before, but with the morning came even more beautiful antique pieces. As they walked down the stairs, they were met by a woman wearing an 1800s maid's outfit. The couple was impressed with the lengths the owners of the bed and breakfast had gone to in bringing the past to life. Chas and Jane spoke to the woman. She averted her gaze and went up the stairs. They were taken aback at the rudeness of the maid and decided to mention her rudeness to the manager.

Chas and Jane reached the dining room where several people, all dressed in the same period costume as the maid, sat enjoying the meal. There was no place setting left for them. Jane told Chas that these must have been the people who'd made the racket that kept them awake all night. Quietly she turned to Chas and told him that she remembered they were supposed to be the only visitors to the house that weekend.

Chas and Jane looked from the crowd of people to one another. Jane tried to talk to the waiter carrying a huge tray of delicious-smelling food to the table. The servant glared at her and turned away without speaking. Jane tried to stop the servant, but when she took hold of the man's sleeve, it dissolved into nothing. Slowly, one by one, the people at the table stood and walked away. They vanished into the dining room walls.

Chas and Jane stood open-mouthed until they heard the creaking and slamming of the back door. They pushed through the dining room door into the kitchen. The minute they saw it was the manager in the kitchen, they were a bit relieved. They questioned the manager about what they'd witnessed. She had no idea what they were talking about. She shrugged off their story and went about fixing their meal. Chase and Jane sat at the table where moments before the ghostly family had been devouring the delicious-smelling food. They ate slowly and wondered about the scene they had observed only moments before.

Finished with breakfast, they left for a day of visiting battlefields and historic sites. In the evening when they returned, Beaufort looked as if it had fallen into disrepair. The manager was nowhere to be found and the house was locked up tight. After the couple finally reached the manager by cell phone, she told them that she thought they were supposed to be there the next day. She told them she would meet them there shortly and let them in the house. Chas and Jane, very confused, decided to go elsewhere for the night.

When the manager finally arrived at Beaufort, she was not the person they met the night before. They retrieved their bags and left. The manager seemed to be a little put out and asked how they had gotten into the house with their luggage in the first place. Chas and Jane tried to explain they'd been there the night before and what had happened. The manager told them that the house had been closed for some time, and no one could have let them inside the night before because she had the only key and had been out of town until earlier that morning. The couple exchanged glances before loading their luggage into the car and driving away. Jane looked back through the car window as they passed under the live oaks in the lane. Beaufort was immediately changed back into the manicured, well-groomed bed-and-breakfast from the day before. Chas and Jane believe they were not welcome at Beaufort because the specters who still live there didn't like strangers always coming and going.

Beaufort rests on the property that once held the Narcisse Prudehomme Plantation. Beaufort was occupied first in the 1700s by the French soldiers who were exploring and trying to protect their claimed land from the Spanish. In 1796, Louis Bartholemy Rachal was given a land grant from the Baron de Carondelet. The land grant included the site of the former Fort Charles. There are remnants of five cisterns in the area where some of the old fort buildings once stood.

Apparently historians can tell this because of their location in proximity to the old house. Their clustered configuration indicates they were used for preserving rainwater that would drain from the rooftops of nearby buildings.

The original house of Beaufort Plantation consisted of one-and-a-half stories. It was made of a mixture of mud and deer hair between cypress timbers, which were moistened, carved, and pegged. It sported four rooms across the front and two large rooms in the rear. No interior corridors existed in this house. Only one room did not open into another. It was called the "stranger room." It enabled the owners to offer their hospitality to travelers in need and not be interrupted by the visiting strangers.

Rachal and his wife Marice François Gillette had lived on the site from 1790 until 1834. When the Rachal heirs had to sell the property to the Narcisse Prudehommes in 1834, the original house was torn down and replaced by the house that stands there now. Upon Rachal's death, he owned nearly twenty slaves who lived at the plantation as well. At the time of his death, ten different men bought the slaves, breaking up the established slave community that Rachal had allowed to grow.

The Prudehommes' fortune began to grow after they acquired the plantation at public auction. By the beginning of the Civil War, the plantation boasted a hundred and twelve slaves. Prudehomme was a fair man and allowed his slaves to accumulate livestock for their livelihood. They worked extra for the privilege.

One of Prudehomme's slaves had sixty chickens and eighteen head of cattle in 1861. His name was Ceraphin. Toward the end of the war in 1864, the Union and Confederate soldiers alike swept through the countryside and wiped out the man's stock. After emancipation, he took the name La-Caze, and a federal court awarded him a settlement of $200 for his loss, and he began life all over. Like many other displaced former slaves, he became a sharecropper .

The Prudehommes remained owners of the property until about 1928, when it was sold again, this time to Mr. Charles Edgar Cloutier. The Cloutiers' son, C. Vernon Cloutier, and new bride, Elizabeth Williams, moved into the house in 1937. Several changes were made to the original house, including opening the stranger's room to the remainder of the house. Rooms were added to the rear of the house. Bathrooms were added in the stairwells, and the stairs to the attic were removed.

Later, in 1944, Cloutier's son bought the property from his widowed mother and three brothers. The property was still owned by descendants of the Cloutier family—Ann Brittain, niece of Elizabeth and William Cloutier, and Jack Brittain. They renamed the plantation in commemoration of Beaufort.

The old plantation house has been sold again to the Badnais family, who do not wish to use the plantation home as a bed-and-breakfast. No longer open to the public, it is now a beautiful and beloved home.

Beaufort is located at 4078 Highway 494 near Natchitoches. Perhaps the ghostly visitors will now be able to rest in peace, since there are no strangers coming and going in their home.

13

FORT JESUP

One man who visited Fort Jesup says he saw a black man carrying a tray of food from the historic kitchen that remains at the fort site. The man weaved in and out between the high stone pillars in front of the original kitchen. Moses returns to Fort Jesup around lunchtime to fix his master's meal. Then he naps for a time before going back to work.

Another man claims he saw Moses bent over the huge opening of the stone fireplace in the kitchen that was once behind the officer's quarters. There was an aura of light all around the old man. When the witness entered the kitchen building, the fireplace was blazing, but the room was freezing cold. Old Moses, who had materialized before his eyes, walked toward the fire. The old man dipped a hearty stew out of the huge black pot hanging in the fireplace. The smell of the cooking food permeated the room, and then the old man left the kitchen, walking toward the stone pillars outside the front door. Sure-footed, the old man carried the hot food. Quietly he vanished into thin air. The square timbered kitchen stayed cold for a short time after the old man left.

One woman was also lucky enough to see the old man. She and a friend walked side-by-side toward the kitchen at Fort Jesup. They walked along, smiling and talking between themselves. As they neared the historic building, she stopped quickly. Her friend didn't see the old man at first. Katy kept trying to tell her friend what she was seeing, but the friend didn't stop talking long enough to hear. Katy says the old man was not watching where he was going. She thought he was about to run into her just before he vanished before her eyes. He was intent on watching the steaming bowl of food he was carrying. The woman shivered as she told her story.

The only surviving building from Fort Jesup was a kitchen. This is the seven-foot-wide fireplace in that kitchen. Some believe that Moses, Zachary Taylor's slave, is still seen using this fireplace to cook for Taylor.

The remains of the fort named after Thomas Sidney Jesup have been restored. Two stone pillars mark the entrance of the old fort. The foundations of thirty or forty buildings were quarried from neighboring hills, and lime masonry was produced from the same source as in the early 1800s. The United States erected the fortress to help establish the western boundary of the state.

In 1819, Spain abandoned all claims to land east of the Sabine River. Following Spain's leaving, the United States established a neutral zone corridor formerly used by outlaws, murderers, and adventurers preying on the tide of Texas-bound emigrants. The fort served as a stronghold for the new frontier. It sat atop a ridge between the Red and Sabine Rivers on the neutral zone also known as the San Antonio Trace.

During the Texas Revolution, Fort Jesup sent troops into the Texas frontier on the pretext of enforcing neutrality laws. In reality, the commander favored annexation and gave material aid to the Texans. Because of popular disapproval, President Jackson ordered the troops back to American soil, keeping the fort in readiness for the upcoming Mexican War.

Lieutenant Colonel Zachary Taylor established the fortress and named it after his good friend Brigadier General Thomas Sidney Jesup. Taylor was loved by his troops and his own personal slaves. One slave, Moses, came with Taylor to the Fort Jesup area. Moses worked alongside the soldiers at the fort and took care of Taylor as well.

The men had to clear the trees along the Red River, cutting timber to build the structures of the large complex. Moses was helping one day and had worked very hard in the steaming hot weather. Being an older man, Moses liked to take a nap in the afternoon before going back to work. Such was the case on that fateful day.

Late that afternoon, Moses rested in one of the half-finished structures. The soldiers, who were assigned field duty, pushed and pulled on the large cross-cut saws clearing out more timber.

A loud yell, "Timber!" rang out across the countryside. Moses, asleep, didn't hear. The tree fell atop the unfinished building, crushing the walls and killing the trusted slave.

Brigadier General Zachary Taylor took command of Fort Jesup in 1844. "Old Rough and Ready" Taylor prepared for Texas's annexation on July 4, 1845, and when the word came, troops were sent by way of New Orleans that resulted in the storming of Chapultpiec. After the Mexican War was over, the fort's importance was over, and in 1846, it was partially abandoned. Only a caretaker and a few guards remained until it was later totally abandoned.

The one original building that remains standing is the kitchen. It stood behind the officer's quarters, of which only the pillars remain. The headquarters building has been rebuilt according to historic plans. It now houses a museum, gift shop, and a dress shop upstairs that sells handmade period clothing.

Interpreters tell the story of Fort Jesup as visitors walk through the site of the officer's quarters and look at the artifacts and the dioramas of renovations of the 1830s, an officer's bedroom, and a barracks cutaway. There is also a display of a stockade hospital. The fort interpreters offer demonstrations of frontier skills on a daily basis.

The kitchen/mess hall, the only truly historic building left on the twenty-two-acre site, is complete with a seven-foot-wide fireplace where the cooking was done. It is a one-story structure made of squared timbers laid one on top of the other with slanted or "waterproof" interlocking joints at each corner. The interior has been furnished in the same fashion as it would have been in the 1840s. The benches and tables of native cypress would have seated about twenty to twenty-five men.

The twenty-two acres of land on display that represents Fort Jesup is only a small portion of the nearly seventeen hundred acres the fort once totaled. To reach these twenty-two acres and the Fort Jesup State Park from the Mansfield Battlefield, turn left onto Highway 175 to Many. At Many, turn onto Highway 6 East. A large brown state park sign is visible from the main road. Turn left at the Fort Jesup sign. The fort is a short distance up the road on the right.

Be aware that in and around the original kitchen the ghost of Lieutenant Colonel Zachary Taylor's manservant, Moses, has been seen taking a tray of food to his master.

14

FORT RANDOLPH

Fort Randolph sits only a few hundred yards from Fort Buhlow. The ghost ship *CSS Missouri* passes by Fort Buhlow and docks across from Fort Randolph. However, the ghost ship is not the only spirit seen by folks in the area. Although there was no fighting at Fort Randolph, some folks say they've seen Lieutenant Colonel Randolph walking around in the hay-field where Fort Randolph once stood.

Jake, an older gentleman who had farmed the field where Fort Randolph stood, abruptly stopped his tractor late one evening. He saw a foggy mist rolling in from nowhere. The closer the fog came, the better he could see what was truly happening. Soldiers marched straight at his tractor. He had never seen anything like them before. The soldiers marched straight *through* his tractor. Parts of the soldiers disappeared into the large wheels as the filmy figures passed through it. Jake waited a few moments before the shock of what he saw wore off. He looked over his shoulder, and there was nothing in the field but him and his tractor. Quickly he started the tractor and went on about his work. At the second round in the field, he came back to the same spot and had to stop again. Becoming unnerved, he hurried his tractor on around the field.

Row after row he cut the hay from the field. At each round, he had to stop and allow the soldiers to march past. They seemed to be deliberately trying to get him to leave the field. At one point the soldiers stopped and knelt, aiming their rifles at him. One of the men stood beside the others, pointing at him and the tractor. The soldier raised his hand as if to give the signal to fire. Jake, unflappable though he thought he was, climbed down from his tractor and hid for a few moments. The soldiers stood and marched away. With only a few more rounds to cut, Jake finished his chore.

Later in the evening he told his wife about the soldiers. The two of them came back to the pasture to see if the soldiers were still marching. They were there. Jake's wife stood watching the soldiers with her mouth open. However, the soldiers were not the main event that evening. As they watched the marching men, Lieutenant Colonel Randolph walked into the field. One minute the colonel was there; the next, he disappeared.

The colonel stood in front of the soldiers shouting orders to straighten their lines and keep their eyes open. The next thing Jake and his wife knew, the colonel stood in front of them, his sword drawn and pointed toward them. They both shivered as an unusually cold wind blew across the field. When the colonel's arm dropped his sword blade, it cut right through Jake like a mist. His voice was gravelly and low. He told them to get out of the field. They were in the way. According to Jake, the colonel's eyes glowed red in the dusky dark light. He and his wife felt threatened and left as quickly as they could.

Jake gave up the lease on the hayfield, and neither he nor his wife ever returned. They both wondered if they were the only ones to see the soldiers at the site.

Fort Randolph was one of three forts planned to keep General Nathaniel Banks from repeating his 1864 Red River Campaign in the Alexandria area. Fort Randolph and one "sister" fort, Fort Buhlow, were completed in March of 1865. Captain C. M. Randolph commanded the troops of the fort. The soldiers at Fort Randolph marched daily, learning how to handle the weapons. They guarded the fort with vigor.

In October of 1864, construction of the fort's earthworks began. It took until March for approximately two thousand men to complete the work, just as the Confederacy began building up defenses in Alexandria against an expected Union attack. The attack never came, but the ironclad *CSS Missouri* was anchored across from Fort Randolph just in case.

The *CSS Missouri* was a center wheel steamer. It floated under the Command of Lieutenant. J. H. Carter. Neither the ironclad nor Lieutenant Carter saw action other than transporting troops and supplies and mining duties. The ship was launched from Shreveport but never got past Alexandria before it was surrendered, sold, dismantled, and laid up in Mount City, Illinois. The *CSS Missouri* was sold at auction in Mount City in November 1865 to John Riley.

On May 26, 1865, General Simon Buckner surrendered the Confederate forces manning both Fort Randolph and Fort Buhlow to Union troops. General Philip Sheridan then occupied both forts on June 2, 1865.

On September 27, 2003, officials met in the hayfield where Fort Randolph once stood to sign papers making the Fort Randolph site a state park. The privately owned site was donated and is now a part of the office of the Louisiana State Parks Department. Several agencies donated approximately $5.5 million to complete this project.

At the Fort Randolph State Park is a visitor's center, an interactive museum, an overlook of Bailey's Dam, and an elevated boardwalk for a tour of the Fort Randolph site. It has a maintenance facility, a manager's residence, roadways, and trails. It is known as the "hub of the Red River Campaign Trail." The park celebrates Fort Randolph, Fort Buhlow, and Bailey's Dam, all instrumental in the Confederates' defense of its capital and all three built in 1864. It is the first state park to be built in Rapides Parish.

Fort Randolph is located about six hundred yards downstream from the O. K. Allen Bridge on U. S. Highway 71. To visit the site at Pineville, turn off Main Street near Lee J's on the Red River levee, then take Riverside Drive northwest to the park. When looking off toward the river, visitors might get a glimpse of the *CSS Missouri* ghost ship.

15

FORT ST. JEAN BAPTISTE

Louis Antoine Juchereau de St. Denis was en route to Mexico from Alabama when he arrived in Louisiana in 1714. He stopped in the area that is now modern day Natchitoches, where he settled and brought civilization to Western Louisiana. He lived out his life at Fort St. Jean Baptiste. Even in death he remains at the fort, buried under the church.

Tim, a tour guide who works at the fort, says that St. Denis still hangs around the fort to make sure no one brings harm to the site.

One of the other guides, Louise, had a large family group come in for a tour of the fort late one afternoon. Dressed in her period costume, she was telling the group the history of the first permanent settlement in Louisiana and all about the fort. She noticed someone else had come into the compound and thought he might go ahead and join the group already taking the tour. The man walked to the church and went inside. Louise assumed the man was going to do the self tour.

She thought at first he looked a little strange; he was dressed in a 1700s costume.

Louise knew she was the only one on duty that late in the day but didn't think any more about it until she finished her tour. When the tour group left her, she thought she should check and see if the man had left the premises, too. She went looking for the mysterious visitor and found no one in the church or around the grounds of the fort. When she checked everywhere for the visitor and couldn't find him, she went to the office at the entrance to the fort and asked if they had seen the gentleman in costume come to the compound or if they had seen him leave. They had not.

Louise is convinced that St. Denis was the man she saw that afternoon. She figures he isn't very happy with all the strangers coming and going in his fort. She thinks he stayed at the fort to make sure no bad elements come

Underneath the church at Fort St. Jean Baptiste is the burial place for the fort's first commander, St. Denis. Some think he still roams the grounds of the fort.

to the place. The fort has been rebuilt only a few hundred yards from the original site based on the original plans drawn by a French engineer named Broutin.

A beautiful African woman has also been seen recently roaming the grounds of Fort St. Jean Baptiste, looking for her children. Ann, who came to Fort St. Jean Baptiste for a reenactment, first noticed the beautiful woman dressed in period costume walking across the compound. Ann approached her to talk with her about the Living History Days events and noticed she was crying. "Where are my children?" she asked, as tears trickled down her cheeks.

Ann tried to put her arm around the woman's shoulder, but she sidestepped and walked away. Ann followed and tried to find out where the children had last been seen so she could help find them. The African woman walked into one of the buildings of the fort. Ann approached and looked inside; it was empty. None of the other reenactors have seen this woman. Ann swears the woman looked like the pictures of Miss Coincoin, who was born to a female slave of St. Denis.

Founded in 1714, Fort St. Jean Baptiste was manned by Louis Antoine Juchereau de St. Denis and a small company of men. The detachment built two huts within the Natchitoches Indian Village on the Red River. This was the first European settlement in the Louisiana territory.

In 1716, Sieur Charles Claude Dustine and a small company of troops from France came to the area to keep the Spanish from Texas from taking over the French territory. Dustine called the outpost Fort St. Jean Baptiste de Natchitoches. The settlement soon became a primary trade center. The Caddo Indians were instrumental in helping to populate the area. The Caddo Indians became so dependent on the French for their provisions that their way of life changed drastically. As far as their material culture was concerned, instead of growing their food as before, they would buy it from the French settlers. The Caddo Indians also relied on the French for clothing and other household needs; instead of hunting and doing for themselves, they bought everything they needed from the French. Fort St. Jean Baptiste thrived under St. Denis, officially appointed commander of the fort in 1722 until he died in 1744.

During his life in Fort St. Jean Baptiste, St. Denis was a slaveholder. Two years before his death in 1744, one of Denis's female slaves gave birth to a baby girl, Marie Therese Coincoin. Marie was sold from the Natchitoches fort where she was raised and had to leave behind four of her children. She then bore ten more children of French-African descent to Thomas Pierre Metoyer and became the founder of a unique colony of people at Melrose Plantation. Marie's children by Metoyer were freed by their father.

French engineer Broutin kept a drawing of the fort and its improvements. In 1732, he was sent by his superiors "to see what had to be done to the fort to put the garrison into security." The fort had been attacked by the Natchez Indians. The changes in the construction of the post made the palisade walls doubly thick, unlike any other colonial urban fortifications. He built crude barracks. Other buildings erected included a church, a warehouse, and a home for the keeper of the warehouse. Just after construction began, the Spanish of Los Adaes complained that the French were invading their territory. St. Denis simply acknowledged the complaint and then ignored it.

Under the French Ministry of the Marine, individual companies garrisoned the fort and carried out administrative and defense duties. The enlisted men were recruited in France, and the officers were aristocratic Canadians. These are the people who helped settle Natchitoches before, during, and after their enlistments.

As of 1762, the military continued to use the fort. The Indians and settlers used it as a commercial trade center. After France was defeated by England, the French government ceded the colony to Spain. The Spanish took over the fortress, and it continued to serve as a trade center. It was also a link to Spain's intracolonial communications. Because it was no longer necessary for the protection of the settlers against the Spanish, the fort was abandoned. By the time the United States assumed ownership of the Louisiana Purchase in 1803, Fort St. Jean Baptiste was no longer habitable. The Americans then built another fort nearby, Fort Claiborne.

Only a few hundred yards from the original site of Fort St. Jean Baptiste, a replica of the old fort has been erected. The replication, based on the original engineer's plans, took months of extensive searching of the archives in Louisiana, Canada, and France. In 1979, Samuel J. Wilson Jr. and the Office of State Parks in Louisiana began building the fort's replica, using the materials and the techniques of the French. Nearly two thousand pine logs were used to form the palisades. Almost two hundred and fifty thousand feet of treated lumber were used in the reconstruction of the fort. Hinges and latches were made at a nearby foundry.

To visit Fort St. Jean Baptiste from Shreveport, travel south on I-49 to Jct. Highway 6 East, then exit to the left into the state park parking lot. Visitors should take note of the cold spots in the fort, especially at the front gate and in the church. There are guided tours daily. Louis Antoine Juchereau de St. Denis may be one of the guides at the fort. He still guards the double-thick walls of his beloved fort and church. The African woman still searches for her children.

The front entrance to Fort St. Jean Baptiste. A specter was captured either leaving the fort or going from one building to another.

16

FORT SELDEN

Killed in a duel with another judge in 1824, Joseph Selden revisits the fort that bears his name. The fort site is on private property, but high school kids have been out to the Bayou Pierre to do whatever it is that teenagers do at night. One group of teens reported that they saw something very spooky near the site of the old fort.

Amy thought her father had found her and her boyfriend at the fort. The sight she saw wasn't her father. Two men came walking out of the misty wooded area around the site. The men walked closer to the car where she and Jimmy sat.

Right in front of the car, the two men stopped and stood facing each other for some time. She heard one of the men yell at the other. "Selden, you are a cad." That's when he pulled off his glove and slapped the other man. Selden's eyes lit up as if they were on fire. In a few minutes they stood back to back. Then they started walking away from each other.

She saw the guns they were holding in the air. She and Jimmy looked at one another, then back at the men. Everything was happening in slow motion. Each man raised his gun. In the distance the two could hear a voice counting slowly. The men walked ten paces and stopped. Each man turned on his heels. One pistol was lowered and aimed only a split second before the other. The blast of fire from the end of the pistol lighted the night slightly. Then the other man's gun fired at the ground as he sank to his knees.

The man called Selden sat propped on his knees for a few moments before he fell face down on the dampened earth. He lay dead. She and Jimmy ran to where they saw the man fall. When they reached the spot, no one was there. There was no one on the ground, no one standing over the man, nothing. The mist began to lift quickly. They searched the area, thinking they may have been mistaken as to where they saw the man fall. They found nothing.

Amy and Jimmy weren't the only young people who saw the horrible duel scene. Others have offered their stories that are basically the same. There should be no other sightings, because the fort site is on private property and no one is allowed to go to the Fort Selden ruins.

The fort was named for Joseph Selden, a native Virginian who served in the Revolutionary War and the War of 1812. He was stationed at Fort Claiborne at Natchitoches and at Fort Selden. He resigned his commission in the army on May 13, 1820. He had been appointed judge of an Arkansas court. He was later killed in a duel with another judge over an insignificant argument. Joseph Selden was never a happy man after he left Louisiana. Friends said he constantly argued with his peers and wished only to come home. After the duel he came home to stay forever.

Fort Selden was established in late 1816 or early 1817. The first correspondence from Fort Selden was dated March 10, 1817. Lieutenant Colonel William A. Trimble, 8th Infantry Commander of the War Department, sent a letter to General E. W. Ripley stating that he understood that the Fort Selden site had been selected by Colonel Selden himself under the command of General Jackson, but it wasn't supposed to be a permanent military post. Some say it was not established until November 1820 by companies of men from the 7th U. S. Infantry. These men were under the command of Lieutenant Colonel Zachary Taylor. He increased the garrison at that time. He explained that any further expenses were to be paid for the barest necessities to keep the troops safe. No other funds were sent to Fort Selden's commander.

In November 1817, more troops were dispatched to Fort Selden under the command of Captains Faulk and Reddy along with the 8th U. S. Infantry. At this time, Colonel Trimble sent a letter to Colonel Butler stating that the property selected for Fort Selden was privately owned. He recommended that the troops be sent back to Fort Claiborne because, in his opinion, Fort Selden was unhealthy for the men. He also mentioned that the stone, hewn timbers, plank boards, and the doors and windows could probably be sold to residents of Natchitoches if the owner of the property would agree.

General Jackson adamantly insisted that the Fort Selden was selected by the War Department and could not be abandoned without official orders. Fort Selden was then reoccupied. A report from the War Department made in 1819 showed Captain W. C. Beard and his command, the 1st Regiment of Infantry, a group of 181 men and Lieutenant H. K. Meade, commander of the 3rd Battalion of Artillery, were stationed at Fort Selden.

Upon his arrival at Fort Selden, Captain Beard advised General Ripley that he had received orders to abandon Fort Claiborne where he had been until May 22, 1819. His orders were sent on June 15, and he was to occupy Fort Selden. Later in July, he received more orders. He was to leave a sergeant's guard at the fort to occupy a position on the Sabine River. Reports show that troops were at Fort Selden throughout 1820 and into 1822.

On March 28, 1822, the commander of the Western Department of the Army, Major General Edmund P. Gaines, was headquartered at Fort Selden. Gaines ordered Colonel Zachary Taylor to move his troops. Taylor was supposed to take his troops to Shields Springs. He was to set up another fort approximately twenty-five miles to the southwest. Gaines reported to the adjutant general about the new fortress in southwest Louisiana, after which he left and never returned.

In 1890, there were remains of the fort. Parts of the walls and some foundations were still visible on the site. About six-tenths of a mile downstream from where the T & P Railroad crosses Bayou Pierre and about 1.3 miles north of Grand Ecore, visitors will find the property where Fort Selden existed. In 1979, the land was owned by Arthur C. Watson and Jack Brittain.

There is nothing left of Fort Selden now except perhaps the spirit of its namesake. Joseph Selden often visits the fort site that was named for him. He seems to always be dueling when he appears.

17

FORT OF THE NATCHEZ

On the western edge of Sicily Island, the sound of musket fire is heard shortly before darkness falls. Afterward, moans are heard. Yelling and high pitched screams echo from the bluffs. Nearby folks think the Natchez Indians who died on the site of Fort of the Natchez are crying out at the injustice of their murder. Others say it is the screams of the dying that are heard.

Thomas, a landowner who lives near the site of the fort, says he has seen strange lights from the old site. The lights turn from green to blue and float just above the ground. He sits on his porch at night and watches the sky toward where the fort once stood. The green and blue circles of misty lights bounce from treetop to treetop along the bluffs.

He heard the sound of muskets firing late one evening, and then the lights went crazy. The orbs bounced here and there and up and down. The yelling and crying he heard was enough to scare any grown man. Thomas shook his head and dug his toe in the ground. He didn't like to admit his fear. He shivered slightly.

The noise got so loud one night he called all his neighbors to see if they knew what was going on. No one else had heard or seen anything. He thought there might have been a gang war or something up on the bluff. The next day, Thomas asked his neighbors to go along to the fort, but they all refused to go up on the bluffs. They had heard the stories of the Natchez Indian ghosts. He went alone to the old fort site, but found nothing, not even an empty casing from a fired gun.

Thomas swore that someone was up there. He thought there were people there with flashlights and guns. Nevertheless, there came a time when he decided not to make the trek up to the bluffs anymore. In the past, he had taken his dogs hunting up on the bluffs, but after a couple of times when the dogs refused to get out of the pickup, he decided it wasn't worth the drive. Besides, there never was any game up there. The sounds and lights aren't really bad except in the winter. Usually in January the sightings get more abundant. But they are there year round.

One evening late in January, Thomas and his wife were coming home from a walk in the crisp winter air just before dusk. Just as they heard the grandfather clock inside the house strike six o'clock, a loud shrill scream rang out across the countryside. They stepped up on their front porch. They looked toward the bluffs and, just as they expected, the lights were dancing. The scream was loud enough to raise the dead or the hair on a frog's back. Thomas reached up and rubbed the back of his neck nervously. Were the Natchez Indians still around?

The Fort of the Natchez was built by the Natchez Indians. The Natchez tribesmen had massacred the French who were settled at Fort Rosalie and had escaped to the eastern side of the Mississippi river in 1729. The tribal warriors established at least one and maybe two forts in the northeast part of Catahoula Parish after their raid on Fort Rosalie.

After the warriors established the Fort of the Natchez, an expedition led by a Frenchman named Perier de Salvert attacked the new fort. Perier de Salvert was the brother of the governor of Louisiana at the time. The Frenchman led an attack on the fort with approximately seven hundred troops. The battle began on January 20, 1731, and ended three days later on January 23. The French captured the Fort of the Natchez and its inhabitants. Most of the warriors who were not killed escaped to fight again another day. The Natchez who were not killed were captured and forced into slavery by the French.

The Fort of the Natchez has been called Fort des Sauvages and also Fort Valeur. The Fort of the Natchez site rests on the property of the Battle Ground Plantation on the western edge of Sicily Island. This plantation was owned by Dr. Henry I. Peck in 1878. On the bluff, entrenchments were seen until after 1824. On the east side of Louisiana Highway 15 between Peck and Sicily Island, there have been many artifacts excavated in recent years. Excavators refuse to go back to the bluffs. They are afraid of the lights that float above the ground at the site of the old fort. When the lights are shining in the darkness, animals stay hidden in their burrows or in the trees. Even the wildlife is afraid of the bouncing lights.

III

Cajun Country

Fort Butler

Yellow Bayou Fort

Fort DeRussy

Fort Butte-a-la-Rose

Niblett's Bluff Fort

Fort Brashear/Fort Star

Fortress Morganza

18

FORT BUTLER

Campers in the area have grown accustomed to battle sounds and the acrid smell of gun smoke, especially during the early morning hours. Jason and several of his friends camped near the site of Fort Butler. As darkness came to the camp, Jason sat at the campfire thinking about the stories he had heard about the fort. Earlier in the day he and his camping buddies had found the common grave of the Confederate soldiers who had died at the fort in a long-ago battle. The horrible odor near the Confederate soldiers' grave had assaulted their nostrils. He hadn't believed the stories he had heard until that afternoon. He sat at the fire remembering the stench of death that permeated the grave.

Later, as Jason slid into his sleeping bag, he thought about how he and his friends had talked about the smells before they turned in for the night. Around one-thirty in the morning he was awakened by the sound of men shouting and screaming. Orders were being shouted to men who were in obvious pain. Shrieks of fear filled the air as well. The sound of cannons and guns being fired rocked the campers' tents. For hours the noises echoed throughout the night.

Jason thought the other men in the camp were playing a prank on him. He got up and checked their tents, but they were all asleep. He was kept awake until about four-thirty when the shouts and sounds of battle became low moans. Finally, at dawn, there were no sounds left in the air except those of the birds greeting the morning. As his friends awakened, he confronted them about his experiences in the night. They all denied having any part in disturbing his sleep. They also denied hearing any of the sounds that he heard.

Jason and his friends stayed only a couple of nights. Each night the same scenes took place, to Jason's private horror. The sounds and smells were always the same, too. He couldn't stand the screams and battle sounds. He could hear the sounds of dying horses as well as of their dying riders, echoing through the night air. His friends didn't know what to do, so the group agreed to cut their camping trip short.

Months later, Jason decided to take his family, including his young sons, to the Fort Butler area. He wanted to work through in his mind what had happened. He also invited his friends to came along. They wanted their old friend to be himself again, so they agreed to the trip. Jason was nervous and still wasn't sleeping much.

While his family and friends busied themselves around the camp, Jason sat in his tent hoping he wouldn't see or hear the same things again. Early in the morning, the smell of death and decaying flesh from the site of the common grave wafted over the campsite. Battle sounds and the acrid smell of gun smoke filled the air. Piercing screams awakened Jason, but this time he was not the only person to see and hear the spirits of Fort Butler; his eldest son also heard the sounds. The battle raged for several hours in the night. Eventually it quieted and the party slept. The next morning, Jason, his family, and his friends left Fort Butler and have not returned.

Built by the Union to protect Donaldsonville, Fort Butler was made of dirt and logs at the mouth of Bayou Lafourche. It was just as important to the Confederates as to the Union. If the Rebels could take Donaldsonville, they could hold the Union Army back. Keeping the Union troops out of the Alexandria area was of the utmost importance to the Confederate Army. If they could keep the Union Army at bay, they could also keep General Banks from reaching Shreveport. Cutting off Banks' communication with New Orleans would be a major coup for the Confederate army. They could continue to fight and perhaps win the war.

In June of 1863, Confederate brigadier general Jean Alfred Mouton sent orders to his two main officers, General Tom Green and Colonel James P. Majors. The orders left no room for doubt: "Take Donaldsonville." The night after the orders were received, General Tom Green moved his troops within a mile and a half of Fort Butler. Louisianans and Texans alike marched together to surround Fort Butler.

General Green allowed his troops to rest for only a short time before moving closer to Fort Butler. After an hour or so, the troops moved in for the attack around one-thirty in the morning. Fighting began immediately.

After the Confederates attacked Fort Butler, they found stake-filled ditches and the lots of tangled natural vegetation in their path. The troops easily overcame the traps and obstacles the Union Army had laid out. When the Rebels came to the sixteen-foot-wide moat, they began having problems. The width of the moat was bad enough, but it was also twelve feet deep. Even if they'd gotten past the moat, the three land sides of the fort were high dirt walls supported by bricks and planking. The river sides of the fort were open, except for stockades that ran down to the water's edge.

A death struggle followed as the soldiers came to the moat. At dawn the Confederates had to pull back. The Union gunboat, *Princess Royal,* aided the Union troops in their quest for victory. The gunboat shelled the Confederate soldiers as they reached the moat. At this point the Confederate soldiers realized they could not win the battle. Taking Fort Butler was a lost

Confederate soldiers left where they died. Photo courtesy of the Opelousas Chamber of Commerce.

cause. Fort Butler and Donaldsonville were to remain under Union rule, but the Confederate soldiers continued to harass the Union soldiers at the fort.

Conflicting reports of casualties include 301 dead Confederate soldiers and 40 Union soldiers. There were 114 wounded and another 107 reported missing. Many of the wounded later died in Union prison camps. When the fighting stopped and the gun smoke cleared, the dead Confederates were tossed into a common grave along with the Union soldiers. At the end of the Civil War, the Union soldiers were removed and buried with full military honors at Chalmette National Cemetery near New Orleans. The Confederates were left in their common grave.

The State of Louisiana has helped to make Fort Butler a historic state park. The United Daughters of the Confederacy continue to work at putting a monument on the grave where the Confederate soldiers lie in eternal sleep.

To visit the site of Fort Butler in Ascension Parish, visitors must drive to Donaldsonville. It is on the north side of Bayou Lafourche across from Donaldsonville where the bayou meets the Mississippi River at Port Barrow. The screams of horror and a raging battle shouldn't frighten anyone who travels there. The men making the sounds are nothing but spirits from a long-ago battle.

19

YELLOW BAYOU FORT

A ghostly woman supposedly from Norwood Plantation can be seen from time to time at Yellow Bayou Fort. Dressed in ragged clothing, she carries trays of food to soldiers. Smells of cornbread, cooked beef, and pork waft across the countryside when the ghostly woman appears. She walks around the area carrying food to the men working on the Yellow Bayou Fort, better known as Fort Humbug 2.

According to one young man, the woman walks back and forth, stopping occasionally. When she stops, the cover on her tray is lifted for a moment, then laid gently back down. Shane says he watched her for nearly thirty minutes one afternoon. She smiled brightly each time she stopped. Her face lit up, and her eyes seemed to twinkle when she stopped and someone took food from her tray. Only when he tried to take her picture did she frown and turn away. He searched for her in his camera view finder. He looked up from his camera, and she was there, but he could never find her through the lens. He took several rolls of film, and his pictures were always empty of her face or form. Although she wasn't recognizable in the pictures, there were bright spots of white in the photographs.

Shane has seen more than just the form of the helpful woman. One evening as he watched her perform her daily walk, a soldier appeared in front of her. The soldier smiled at the woman and spoke something Shane couldn't hear. As he stepped closer, the woman turned toward him and glared at him with reddened eyes. Shane continued to watch the two apparitions. Suddenly, she and the soldier faded away.

On another afternoon, Shane walked around the area where Yellow Bayou Fort once stood. He followed the ghostly woman for quite some time. As he followed her, she would turn and look over her shoulder at him. She would smile coyly and walk on just in front of him. At one point he saw her stumble and nearly fall. She regained her balance and continued on her way. He thought someone had reached out to catch her. The tray hit the ground, but there was nothing scattered, and there was no sound. They walked about three miles before she stopped abruptly. The look of horror on her face caused Shane to stop and look closer at the scene unfolding in front of him. The woman dropped to her knees and covered her face with her hands. Shane heard a whip crack and saw blood appear on her back. Several times the whip lashed out and more blood oozed from her flesh. Quickly she vanished into the never-never land of the beyond. She had led Shane to the area where the Norwood Plantation's slave quarters had once stood. Shane wondered if this woman might be connected in some way with the Norwood or Old Oak Plantation.

No one has answered his questions. No one seems to know the young woman. She apparently has come to feed the soldiers and is punished for her work.

Some folks in the area believe that there never was a fort at Yellow Bayou, but there was a complex of forts at Yellow Bayou and Bayou des Glaises. These forts were built during the Civil War. The earthen breastworks were much the same as other fortifications in the state. The purpose of these forts and earthworks near the village of Simmesport was to prevent the Union troops from invading Central Louisiana.

Construction on Yellow Bayou Fort and its earthworks began on December 15, 1863. The troops from Walker's Texas Division and Scurry's Brigade worked on the fort in shifts. Scurry's Brigade camped near Bayou des Glaises in the abandoned slave quarters on the Norwood Plantation. They took four-hour shifts seven days a week and worked under miserable conditions. The weather never seemed to cooperate with the soldiers or the builders. One day it was rainy; the next day, the heat was so unbearable that they had to lie around to keep from having heat strokes. They ate tolerably on what they found at the plantation—cornbread, poor beef, sugars, and molasses. The soldiers were supplied on occasion with pork, potatoes, and flour by the military. Even though the soldiers were well fed, they resented having to work so hard on a fortress they felt would be useless to the Confederacy.

Several letters from husbands to wives have been found. One in particular from Dr. Edward Cade, a surgeon for Walker's Texas Division, related that the command was engaged in throwing up quite an extensive line of works. He felt that the labor of the men was merely thrown away as the earthworks were utterly useless. Other letters were written to the same effect.

Fort Humbug 2/Yellow Bayou Fort had other problems as well. The Southern flank of the fort's defense was an impassable swamp during the wet season. During the summer months or other times when all was dry, soldiers could march right across the swamp with no trouble. In March of 1864, the weather had been unseasonably dry for a long period of time and the swamp was passable. This left the fort vulnerable to attack by the Union Army.

The 36th Texas Cavalry fought several engagements in Louisiana during the Red River Campaign. They skirmished on a day-to-day basis with Bank's troops from mid-March 1864 until the end of May. From Monett's Ferry to Norwood's Plantation, the Texas Cavalry fought these same troops over and over. On May 17, 1864, Companies A and B from the 4th joined the 36th at Norwood's Plantation.

The following day, the Confederates suffered heavy losses at Yellow Bayou Fort, and the Union Army pushed through to Simmesport. At this point, the Confederates abandoned Fort Humbug 2, which was still unfinished.

Colonel George D. Robinson and his troops arrived at Yellow Bayou on May 17 and built a bridge for the Union troops to use to cross the bayou. He came upon two formidable earthworks on the west bank of the bayou. His orders were to take and totally destroy the works.

The larger of the forts was destroyed, but the other fort further south, probably Yellow Bayou Fort, escaped destruction. On May 18, after the continuous Confederate harassment of Bank's troops, Banks learned that Major General Richard Taylor's force was camped near Yellow Bayou. Banks proceeded to order Brigadier General A. J. Smith to stop the Rebel general. Smith, unable to do as ordered, sent Brigadier General Joseph A. Mower to face Taylor's troops. Mower's troops drove the Confederates to the main line. Once more the Rebels came back full force. The Federals were forced to give ground. A seesaw action continued for several hours. When the ground cover caught fire, both sides quit.

The Union retired from the battle at the Yellow Bayou Fort, ending the Red River Campaign that Banks had started. Banks had made good his threat to crush the Confederates. The Union Army hadn't lost nearly as many men, and they could return to the main body so the Northern forces could fight more efficiently as a whole army. A total of 860 men lost their lives in the battle of Yellow Bayou. The list of dead included 360 Union troops and 500 Confederate troops.

Yellow Bayou Fort stood its ground under several different names. First it was called Fort Humbug 2 because the soldiers who worked on it for so long thought it useless. The Union called it Fort Humbug 2 as well as Fort Scurry, Fort Taylor, Fort Lafayette, Fort Morgan, and Fort Carroll at various times.

To visit the Civil War Park at Simmesport is a great experience. Only a small section of the original Yellow Bayou Fort still exists. The remains can be seen on the south side of Louisiana State Highway 1. The area is just west of Simmesport. Perhaps a glimpse of the fort will also bring an encounter with the woman who feeds the soldiers from long ago. These soldiers died in battle before they finished the job they started. Perhaps they still hang around the park area to complete the fort.

20

FORT DERUSSY

Leon strolled along the old channel of the Mississippi and the edge of Fort DeRussy. The trees slowly began to fade away. He stopped abruptly and turned to the sound of cannon fire whizzing past his head. The next thing he knew, he was lying on his stomach in the dirt. Someone had hit him from behind, knocking him down.

Leon got to his feet quickly and looked to see who had hit him in the back. A man dressed as a Confederate soldier lay on the ground. Blood soaked into the dirt. Leon knelt to the man's side and gently turned him over on his back. Leon judged the young man to be in his late teens. He shook his head at the loss of such a young life. He tore the soldier's shirt off and ripped it in two pieces. The man's face was bloodied almost beyond recognition. His eyes fluttered in near death. He no longer had a nose. The sight of his head and face sickened Leon. Quickly, he wrapped the top of the man's head in the shirt trying to stop the bleeding and to keep from having to see the horrible sight. He dragged the soldier from the center of the old trench.

Again the sound of shells from the river burst nearby. Cannon fire was followed by rifle fire. Leon stayed low, crouching by the soldier's side, and noticed the captain's bars on the man's uniform. Leon sat watching as the man's eyes sprang open, and Leon asked him what was happening. The man looked confused, but uttered two words: "War man." Leon asked his name but got no reply. He left he man lying on the ground to go for help.

Leon heard yelling and screaming. About halfway across the center of the compound, armed men ran toward him. One of them, dressed as a Federal soldier, was about to run him through with a bayonet. Leon froze on the spot. He couldn't move at all. About the time the soldier lunged, he vanished into thin air. Leon couldn't believe what was happening. He hurried back to where he had left the fallen captain. There was no one to be found. He searched the area, looking for the man but to no avail. Trees towered above the breastworks of Fort DeRussy, between and on top of the entrenchments. The birds sang in the trees where only moments before he could have sworn he heard cannon fire. None of what he'd seen was still there.

Leon still goes for walks at the Fort DeRussy site. Bits and pieces of the scene often unfold as he meditates. He knows of no one else who might have witnessed the same things along the breastworks of the fort. Three miles north of Marksville, Fort DeRussy gallantly stood with its Confederate builders inside. Colonel Louis G. DeRussy, the fort's namesake, commanded a regiment of troops in the Mexican War before he was made commander of the 2nd Louisiana Regiment of volunteers early in the Civil War. General Taylor appointed Colonel DeRussy to build the defense works on the Red River. Its purpose was to keep Federal ships from traveling upstream to Alexandria. In 1864, Fort DeRussy was enlarged.

Because part of the fort was under water in May of 1863, the Federal navy and land forces attempted to approach the unfinished fortress. To avoid the impending Union attack, Captain Kelso took his Confederate gunboats, the *Grand Duke* and *Cotton,* downriver from Alexandria to Fort DeRussy. The mission was to remove any armament from the fort that the Federals might be able to use. The troops manning the ships retrieved several cannons before the Federal gunboats *Albatross, Arizona,* and *Estrella* forced the Confederates and Captain Kelso to withdraw.

Several days later, the Federals sent troops ashore to destroy Fort DeRussy. They demolished several cannons, but the Union soldiers didn't have enough powder to blow up the main works of the fort, so it was left intact. Sometime later, Confederate troops returned and made improvements on Fort DeRussy.

The Federals attacked Fort DeRussy once more with Colonel William F. Lynch's 1st Brigade. These troops were assisted by Colonel William T. Shaw's 2nd Brigade of Brigadier General Joseph A. Moyer's 3rd Division and Major General A. J. Smith's 16th Corps. About four o'clock in the afternoon on May 14, 1864, the shooting began at the fort. By six-thirty that same afternoon, the Confederates had surrendered.

The Rebels lost five soldiers and had four wounded. The Union lost three men with thirty-five wounded. There were 317 Confederate soldiers taken prisoner at the end of the day. Of the prisoners taken, twenty-five were officers. Most of the men taken captive were from Texas. Twenty-nine men were from the Crescent Regiment, and thirteen were taken from the St. Martin Battery. The remaining men were from various other Texas units.

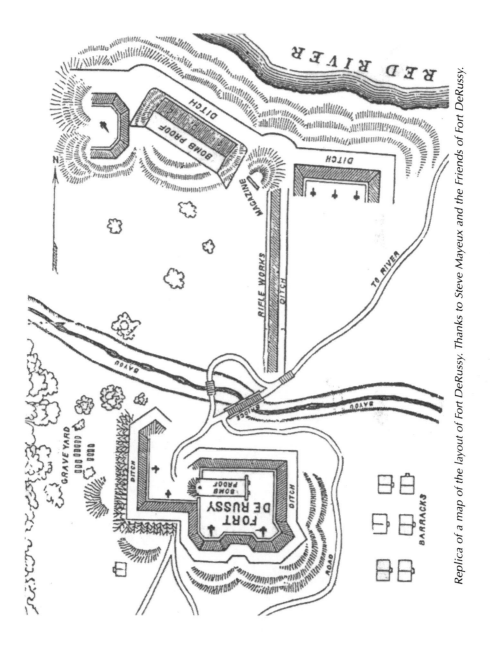

Replica of a map of the layout of Fort DeRussy. Thanks to Steve Mayeux and the Friends of Fort DeRussy.

After seizing the fort, the Federal troops took the armaments out of the fort and destroyed them. The ammunition magazines were also destroyed. The soldiers cut ditches through the breastworks and shot three solid shots through the iron casements of the fortress walls. Because of the damage done to Fort DeRussy in that final battle, it was used afterward only as a picket station by the Union. Fort DeRussy was once believed to be impregnable, but it fell and opened the Red River from the fort to Alexandria for the Union army.

Visits to Fort DeRussy are scheduled for a small admission fee by the Friends of Fort DeRussy. Once visitors are at Fort DeRussy they can walk the grounds or simply meditate under the huge trees or in the trenches. If visitors happen to start hearing loud noises, they shouldn't be alarmed. The soldier who saved a life and was shot in the face may be around to save them.

21

FORT BUTTE-A-LA-ROSE

Smoke filled the air in St. Martin Parish on Cow Island as Sammy drove to Fort Butte-a-la-Rose. The smoke thickened so much as she approached the stronghold site that she could hardly see the road. Choking from the smoke, she finally reached the site and pulled to a stop. The smoke lifted enough to reveal flames licking the air from the site where the barracks buildings had burned long ago. No brush was on fire. None of the other buildings were burning. Sammy saw nothing but smoke and flames where the barracks once stood. The flames danced in mid-air, and the smoke billowed out over the island just above the ground. The sight of flames above the ground scared her at first. The flames reminded her of the northern lights in Alaska, except for the colors and the smoke.

As Sammy stepped out of her car, the flames and the smoke cleared away in the duration of a heartbeat, as if by magic performed by some invisible person. The clearing smoke frightened her, and she thought about returning to her vehicle, but she knew she had to finish teaching her students about the fort. She looked around at the Fort Butte-a-la-Rose site. The history of the Civil War she'd studied didn't teach her much about this particular fort. She wanted to know more about the fort and the men who had served there. She needed to see the fort up close, to experience the smells of the land, the feel of the air; most of all she hoped to find artifacts that would tell her how the men lived while at the fortress.

Sammy stepped up to the long, empty building where the powder magazine once held ammunition. Inside, she drew in her breath. Standing in the middle of the magazine were several Confederate soldiers. She thought she was alone at the fort. She didn't expect to see reenactors. One soldier held a fairly long length of fuse rope. Each of them smiled sheepishly. Sammy started toward them, expecting that reenactors could tell her a lot about the fort, but they turned and walked past her to the door. She thought the men rude until she turned to see them vanish into the dusky air outside. Confused, she tried to clear her mind about what she had seen. Finally she began taking notes and recording what she saw.

Before darkness completely enveloped the island, Sammy set out to leave. She hadn't found what she came for, but what she did find was well worth the trip to the island. While driving away from Fort Butte-a-la-Rose, Sammy looked in her rearview mirror. The flames started burning again. The light from the fires guided her down the eleven-mile road back to St. Martinsville.

Out on the west end of Cow Island where the Atchafalaya River meets Cow Island Bayou and Bayou à la Rose, the river ends and the bayous join. Fort Butte-a-la-Rose was built in 1863, and stood until it was partially burned later the same year.

The Federal Navy, under the command of Lieutenant A. P. Cooke, got information from an informant about the armaments at the fort. According to the informant, Fort Butte-a-la-Rose was well armed. The man told the lieutenant that the commander of the fort was Burbank, a gunner from the *CSS Cotton* of the Confederate Army. The informant told about the three large cannons that protected the fort. The crew of the *CSS Cotton* was supported by five companies of infantrymen. Based on the information, Lieutenant Cooke made up his mind to attack the fort.

Major General Richard Taylor took charge of Louisiana's Defense on August 20, 1862. Courtesy of the Daily World *and the Opelousas Chamber of Commerce.*

According to a report from General Richard Taylor, the guns mounted at the fort were placed there with much hard labor and the loss of a couple of lives. He was ready to defend the fortress at any cost. On December 31, he had been sent to get the fort ready, and it took him until February 20, 1863, to carry out his orders. He also reported to his superiors that he had the backup of Company F of the Crescent Regiment.

Fort Butte-a-la-Rose, also known as Fort Burton, was in the way of General Nathaniel P. Banks of the Federal Army. The Yankee general ordered one of his officers, General William H. Emory, to get his forces together and seize the fort. General Emory and approximately three thousand troops struck out to take Fort Butte-a-la-Rose. However, Emory and his troops, blocked by debris at the junction of the two bayous, were unable to reach the fort.

In the spring of 1863, four Federal gunboats forced the surrender of Fort Butte-a-la-Rose. The *Clifton, Calhoun, Arizonan,* and *Estrella* gunboats were commanded by Lieutenant Commander Augustus P. Cooke. He and his men and boats were supported by several companies of the 16th New Hampshire Infantry Regiment. On April 20, they captured sixty of the soldiers of the Crescent Regiment. Two cannons were also impounded and destroyed.

The infantrymen from the 16th New Hampshire Regiment stayed on at the fort until May 30, 1863. At this time, the men dismantled the breastworks and burned the nine barracks buildings. The magazine building survived the blasting and fire of the Federals because some of the Rebels, who escaped capture, sneaked back in the fort and put out the fuse.

Fort Butte-a-la-Rose is located south of Interstate 10 in St. Martin Parish at the junction of Cow Island Bayou and Bayou-a-la-Rose just off State Highway 352. At the junction of Farm Road 3177, any visitor can see the remains. The powder magazine still stands guard over the ruins of the fort. Confederate soldiers who keep a watch for lit fuse rope are still at the fort. If a visitor is lucky enough, smoke might fill the air and visions of the past may appear.

22

NIBLETT'S BLUFF POST

Thirty men gathered around a campfire. Laughing and joking, one by one they turned in the direction of the light that illuminated their faces. Each man was covered in red splotches from measles. The men walked to a palm-covered building where they disappeared. In the moonlight the palm buildings themselves dissolved into nothingness.

A troop of boy scouts had camped out in the Niblett's Bluff State Park to earn their badges. They sat around the campfires telling stories after their supper. The leaders sent the boys to bed and had started to their own tents when they observed a group of men through a heavy haze. They were dressed in Texas cavalry uniforms. They sat around the same campfire the young boys had just vacated. The leaders stood watching the ghostly-looking men for a time before they started toward the fire. The head leader, Kelly, spoke to the men, warning them to move on out of the area as they were intruding on the Boy Scout Camp and no strangers were allowed. One of the apparitions stood and turned toward Kelly. The man's eyes seemed to be ablaze. Sweat formed on his brow, and his face was covered in measles. The man looked miserable.

Kelly and his companion backed away from the frightening sight. As they stood apart from the group, the ghostly men at the fire turned toward the woods and walked away. The men were all covered in the measles. As they watched the phantom-like men fade into the woods, the leaders looked at one another and blinked rapidly, trying to believe what they saw. They went to the tent they shared, and both sat at the opening watching and waiting.

The night wore on, and their wait was rewarded. The men with the measles congregated at the campfire once more. Each man turned as if to warm his back.

"Attention!" The shout from the circle of campfire light drew their attention. From the darkness another light-shrouded figure appeared. The soldiers snapped to attention and lined up side by side. Another shout, "March!" and the figure in front of the soldiers began walking toward the woods. One by one the soldiers followed, marching along in an aura of light until they vanished into the wooded perimeter of the fort site. After they had taken a step or two, the men felt their foreheads and covered their eyes. Some grabbed their stomachs and bent forward. Their moans of pain grew louder as they marched into the darkened woods.

The next morning, the leaders rousted the boys from their sleeping bags and did not mention to them what they had seen. However, one of the boys asked who the men were at the previous evening's campfire. The leaders refused to discuss the events of the night before.

Measles was one of the diseases that plagued the Southern soldiers. Several companies of men were lost to the red, splotchy disease. Many times the measles broke out among the troops in the summer months. Sibley's Texas Brigade, or at least part of it, was doing duty at Niblett's Bluff in May of 1863. While stationed at the the Post of Niblett's Bluff, the 1st Texas Cavalry built a house of palms. The troops wintered at the Post of Niblett's Bluff between 1863 and 1864. They built the breastworks during the early part of 1863. Colonel A. Buchel commanded the Texas troops while they built the fortress. Another company of Texans under the command of George O'Bryan was also stationed at the Post of Niblett's Bluff. These men were at the fort in the summer of 1863. While they were helping to erect the breastworks, they contracted the measles and died before they finished their work. They were promptly buried in unmarked graves at the Post of Niblett's Bluff.

In 1958, chapters of the Louisiana and Texas United Daughters of the Confederacy placed a granite marker at the Niblett's Bluff site. The thirty soldiers who died of that dreaded disease will now be forever remembered. To see this beautiful marker, visitors can travel to Calcasieu Parish on the east side of the Sabine River. It is about five miles north of Interstate Highway 10 at the Niblett's Bluff State Park.

Campers at the state park may be awakened in the night by marching soldiers with the measles. The men must practice, but they don't feel well. Sometimes they stand in front of campfires to warm their souls. They are only guarding the fort.

23

FORT BRASHEAR/FORT STAR

While visiting Brashear, Desmond searched out the site of old Civil War fortification markers. As he stood reading the information on the sign, he noticed several other men gathering around him and the sign. He didn't think anything about it at first, because there were always other people at these sites. Desmond looked closer at the men who were huddled near him.

Within minutes, fifty or more men stood at the marker, staring at nothing. Desmond thought it was strange that the men were dressed in Civil War uniforms. Three of the men wore Confederate uniforms, and the remaining men wore the blue uniforms of the Union. The soldiers milled about as if they were lost. Desmond noticed something even stranger about the soldiers. Their tattered and torn clothing was stained with blood. Some had only a few stains, while others were covered in blood. Many of the men's faces were marred by bullet holes, and others were so messed up it was hard to even see a face. Having worked in hospital administration and served in the Korean War, Desmond knew what battle wounds looked like. These men had been in a great battle.

Startled, Desmond started to leave the site. As he stepped out of the circle of men, he was met by a gentleman in a Union officer's uniform. Judging from the brass on the bodice of his uniform, Desmond figured the man was a lieutenant commander. Looking dazed and confused, the Union officer approached Desmond, and that is when Desmond saw the bullet hole in the middle of the man's forehead. A trickle of blood oozed from the hole.

Desmond rubbed his eyes as if to wipe away the madness he was seeing. He turned away from the officer and the men standing at the marker to see where his wife had gone off to. He wanted to know if she was seeing the same things he saw. He saw her a short distance away from the marker. When he turned back to the marker, the men were gone. Desmond was the only person there. He called his wife over and asked her if she had seen the men. She had not seen anything except the marker.

For the rest of the day, they discussed what Desmond had seen, and why the soldiers had revealed themselves to him. The only reason they came up with was that the spirits of the men felled in battle still hang around the last place they lived because it was also the place they died. As Desmond and his wife drove away from the Fort Brashear/Fort Star marker, a Rebel victory yell filled the air around them.

Fort Brashear/Fort Star was built by Union forces to protect them from the Confederates and the sympathizers in and around Brashear and St. Mary Parish. It was the largest of five earthen fortifications in the area. The Union built Fort Brashear/Fort Star more specifically to keep control of the Atchafalaya River and Bayou Teche.

After the surrender of New Orleans to the Union Navy in April 1862, Baton Rouge fell to Yankee control in late May. Next was the destruction of Donaldsonville in August. The town was practically ruined by the Yankee gunboats. Later in the fall, General Godfrey Weitzel made his way into Lafourche Parish. On October 29, 1862, Lieutenant Commander Thomas Buchanan ordered his Yankee troops and their gunboats onto the Atchafalaya River.

Rebel Brigadier General Jean Alfred Mouton and his troops made it across the river away from Fort Brashear/Fort Star to Berwick with one gunboat. The *CSS Cotton,* commanded by Captain E. W. Fuller, handed out a large amount of damage to one of the Yankee gunboats. Like a fine lady, the *CSS Cotton* made a graceful exit from the battle and went upstream to Bayou Teche.

On November 2, the *CSS Cotton* and her four Yankee opponent gunboats met once more, this time in the bayou. Captain Fuller got Buchanan's gunboats in his sights and opened fire. The battle raged for three days, and the *CSS Cotton* came out the victor, allowing General Mouton and his men time to gather more troops. Later that week, General Richard Taylor recommended Fuller for a promotion because of his heroism against overwhelming odds.

Nathaniel Banks took over command of the Union army in Louisiana from General Butler. He urged his superior, General Weitzel, to allow him to press on westward. On January 13, 1863, Banks sent Buchanan's gunboats to Cornay's Bridge. This was the last battle for the Rebel boat *CSS Cotton.* It burned to the waterline. The *CSS Cotton* was not the only fatality that night. Yankee commander Buchanan was shot in the head and died instantly. The battle victory, however, belonged to the Union forces.

Brigadier General Alfred Jean Mouton was one of the bravest and most brilliant officers in the Confederate Army. He was also the youngest. The original portrait of General Mouton hangs in the museum at the Historic Mansfield Battlefield Site.

Following these battles, Fort Brashear was built. Union soldiers built a triangular fort from the mouth of the Atchafalaya River to the Bayou Boeuf and back to the railroad tracks. The Union Army also built breastworks on a smaller scale and named it after Buchanan.

Later in March 1863, a Union gunboat steamed full speed ahead into Confederate waters. The *Diana* ran into problems when the Rebel sharpshooters opened fire on her. After three hours of slaughter, the *Diana* caught fire and became a floating morgue for the Union soldiers aboard. There were no survivors from the gunboat.

General Banks, in retaliation for the slaughter of the crew of the *Diana*, brought eighteen thousand troops to Fort Brashear/Fort Star. The troops began marching after the fifteen hundred Confederate troops at Fort Bisland. The Yankees attacked the Texas and Louisiana troops at ten o'clock in the morning on April 12, 1863. General Mouton's troops held off the Yankees until they were reinforced by Dick Taylor's troops on April 14.

Several weeks passed as the Rebels retreated and the Union followed, plundering everything in their path. Determined to best the Yankees once and for all, General Taylor led them on a merry chase right back to Fort Brashear/Fort Star and St. Mary Parish. One late night in June, the sneaky Confederates positioned cannons on the Berwick side of the river. The next night, June 22, 1863, darkened slowly, and the Confederates began crossing the river. They used their bateaux, sugar coolers, and pirogues to get them across. Once landed on the Brashear side of Lake Palourde, they lay low until dawn of June 23. At the first sight of light, the Rebel yell surprised the Union soldiers still in their bedrolls. The Union lines of defense were destroyed, and the men ran around confused and unable to fight back. At the end of the battle, the Rebels had lost only three men as opposed to the forty-six listed dead on the Union side. The Confederate soldiers captured Fort Brashear/Fort Star and over one thousand soldiers.

The marker for Fort Brashear/Fort Star is located on 4th Street off Highway 90 in Morgan City. Visitors to the former fort site and marker often hear a Rebel yell early in the morning. Others see General Buchanan and other troops milling around the sign.

24

FORTRESS MORGANZA

As visitors to Morganza drive by the fields of sugarcane and the swamps of Pointe Coupee Parish, sometimes shadows are seen lurking in those cane fields. Not many people pay much attention to those shadows anymore, but one young lady who was out for a ride on her horse late one February afternoon paid close attention. Rebecca's horse spooked as they passed one of the cane fields. She tried to calm the animal, but it continually pranced sideways. Rebecca looked around for what might make the horse shy so badly. There, in among the cane stalks, was a man crouched low to the ground. The man waved his arms angrily at her as if to wave her away from his hiding place.

Rebecca shrugged her shoulders and nudged the horse forward. Her horse pranced around, shying from the cane waving in the wind again. She looked closer, and there was another man lying on his stomach with a rifle pointed toward her. She yelled at the man to go away. He looked up at her and vanished into thin air. She wondered what was going on, but there was no one to ask now. She rode back to the spot where she had seen the first man, and he was gone too. Rebecca rode her horse on down the edge of the field and saw nothing else.

Her ride back home, however, was a different story. She rode along at an easy canter. Before she knew what happened, three men jumped out from the cane field and stood pointing rifles at her. She pulled the horse to an abrupt halt and sat watching them closely, holding her breath. One of them motioned for her to get off the horse. She refused. Another one came to her stirrup and reached up to grab her. As he did, she kicked out at him. Her foot went right through his chest. Surprised, she jabbed the horse with her heels, and it jumped forward right on top of the other two men. She rode off at a gallop. When she turned in the saddle to look back, there was no one where she had been stopped.

These are not the only apparitions to be seen in Morganza. Harold reported seeing several black men using wooden shovels to dig trenches. They were pitching the dirt into giant mounds. He wondered what the men were supposed to be building. He stopped his car and got out to talk to them. None of them even looked up from the work. He tried again to talk to the men, but they just kept on working. When he approached one of them and touched his shoulder, the man stared at him angrily and disappeared. The others looked up then and also faded into nothingness. One of the soldiers was wearing a blue uniform with one stripe on the arm. Harold felt he knew that these men were from one of the colored regiments who served the Union Army stationed at Fortress Morganza under the command of General Banks.

General Nathaniel P. Banks failed to take the Red River for the Union. Upon this disaster for the Union Army, Banks directed his troops to Morganza, where they camped. At Morganza the general instructed his troops to build a fortress for their protection. The earthen breastworks served the Union Army well throughout the remainder of the war.

On September 29, 1863, after the Fortress Morganza was built, Banks took his troops on maneuvers toward Bayou Fordoche, where he thought the Confederates were holed up. They met the Confederate troops at Stirling Plantation in a battle since called the "largest Civil War engagement in Pointe Coupee Parish." The Union Army limped back to Fortress Morganza to wait for reinforcements.

On May 22, 1864, the Ninety-ninth Colored Infantry arrived at Fortress Morganza. They enjoyed a few days' rest after the forced labor and marching since April 18th from Alexandria.

Upon their arrival to Fortress Morganza, the troops of the Ninety-ninth discovered that because of his failure in the Red River Campaign, General Banks had been replaced as commander and the new commander in charge, Brigadier General Emory, had taken over at the fort.

The colored infantry troops were almost immediately put to work at hard labor. The new commander wanted the fortress strengthened. In June of 1864, the Ninety-ninth Regiment was taken off army duty and put to work as carpenters and bricklayers. This action by the commanding officer had negative effects. Lieutenant Hughes, officer in charge of the Ninety-ninth Regiment, was disgusted with the way Emory was demoralizing the troops. Hughes felt that he and his troops were doing way too much manual labor, and he felt it was because of the troops being colored. Many of the officers of the regiment handed in their resignations. They wanted no part of General Emory's new rules and regulations. They asked for immediate and unconditional release from the army. They felt he was prejudiced and no better than the plantation owners they had fled from. These resignations were quickly refused by General Emory.

The colored troops of the Ninety-ninth Regiment never received the recognition they deserved. Lieutenant Hughes was livid when he read the official reports on the Red River Campaign. The commander of the Union fleet, Admiral Porter, never once even mentioned the hard labor of the regiment. These regiments of colored troops worked day and night before the gunboats reached the rapids. The men of the Ninety-ninth Regiment worked with two other regiments of engineers to bring the naval vessels over the rapids in the river, and they brought them to safety.

The Ninety-ninth Colored Infantry Regiment was set to fortifying the cannon positions at Fortress Morganza for several months. The leaders of these troops had to fight off boredom and the troops themselves had to fight off the urge to run away from the same treatment they had been receiving at their plantations. Lieutenant Hughes complained to his superiors, and he and the regiment were finally allowed four days of leave. Starting on July 3, 1864, the troops left Fortress Morganza and traveled to New Orleans. Most of the troops went to see their families who were kept in the city. While the troops were in New Orleans, there was an outbreak of yellow fever. Hundreds of cases were reported in the city alone. The epidemic lasted from August to September. Fear of the disease spreading kept the regiment close to Fortress Morganza, except for those who contracted it in New Orleans.

During the epidemic, there was a lot of time spent in recruiting soldiers, mostly blacks. Military action was pretty quiet except for the mustering in of the new recruits and a few skirmishes. Some of the regiments received orders to go elsewhere as they were needed.

The Sixty-second Regiment Infantry left Fortress Morganza. On September 6 orders were received and the regiment retired from the fortress to gather at Bayou Sara. They weren't replaced at Fortress Morganza until February 23, 1865, when the Sixty-first Regiment Infantry was ordered to the fort.

Soon after the Sixty-first Regiment joined the troops at Fortress Morganza, a skirmish broke out between a small band of Confederate soldiers and the Union Army at Grosse Tete near Morganza. The Rebel soldiers outsmarted the Yankees by hiding in the swamps and sugarcane fields. The Union cavalry was defeated and started back to Fortress Morganza. The

Rebel troops lay low and waited for the Union soldiers to leave. The Confederates followed them back to the fortress in Morganza and took over the camp for a short time.

Deep in the heart of Pointe Coupee Parish is the little community of Morganza. Memories and the ghosts of the brave Confederate soldiers and their Union counterparts who manned Fortress Morganza are all that remain of the fort.

IV

Plantation Country

Fort Tunica

Fort Desperate/Port Hudson

Fort San Carlos

Baton Rouge Arsenal

25

FORT TUNICA

Steve fished in the Old River almost every day. One afternoon in June, he began hearing strange noises from the wooded area around the river bend. The water became still and glassy smooth. Not one to give up easily, he continued to watch the bobber on the end of his fishing line. Nothing came near his hook. Steve knew something was wrong, because he had always caught his limit of fish from his favorite spot on the river. However, that day the fish stayed away.

Once he thought the bobber went under the water, but just as he started to reel in his fish, the noise from the woods started again. This time the noises—screams and cries—became louder than the last time. Frustrated, Steve pulled in his line and laid his pole on the bank. He strolled to the edge of the woods in search of the sounds he kept hearing. It sounded as if someone was moaning in pain. He felt he needed to help whoever was hurt in the woods.

A short way into the depths of the brush, Steve couldn't hear the moans anymore. Whoever was in there must have passed out or died. The thought of finding a dead body in the woods began to frighten him. After searching for quite a while, he gave up. He never found anything. Steve left the woods and the river to go for help. Some friends came back with him, but none of them could find the source of the moans and cries.

Steve's friends teased him about perhaps having a little too much to drink while he was fishing. He protested that all he had in his cooler was soda pop and a bologna sandwich. Laughing and slapping Steve on the back, his friends quit suddenly as the strange moans and cries for help began again in earnest. The three men searched the woods. A strange mist oozed from the ground as they combed the area. War chants rang out through the tall trees, causing the birds to hush their singing. Cries of pain and suffering soon filled the airwaves, and the war chants died away. They all searched again but never found any evidence of a human or animal that might be making the noises.

Steve has fished the Old River many times since that first incident. At times he hears the moans and cries; other times he doesn't.

On April 24, 1716, an entrenchment with stakes and posts was built just across the Old River from the Tunica Indians' village. It included three cabins, a storehouse, a guardhouse, and a jail. The Frenchman Bienville had talked to the Tunicas, and they told him this would be a good site for his fort because it never flooded. In June of 1716, the island was covered in a foot of water. This may have been the reason that Bienville later moved the fort to the site where Fort St. Joseph stood in the village of the Tunicas.

After the Natchez Indians went on the warpath and massacred the French garrison and the settlers at Natchez on November 29, 1729, the French made an agreement with the Tunicas. They would help the Tunicas protect their families, and in return the French would be able to live with the Indians for their own protection as well. On December 10, 1729, a letter was sent to Sieur de Marvillaux telling him to go to the village of the Tunicas. He led a detachment of French soldiers and settlers. They fortified the village to help prevent a surprise attack by the Natchez Indians. Eight days later, M. De Louboey, the French commander at New Orleans, arrived at the village with an additional twenty-five men. These men, along with the Tunicas and Choctaws, were to march against the Natchez Indians, but they had to build a palisade to protect the Tunicas' women and children. During that time, Captain Ignace Droutin reported to his superior that he and his men and the settlers were in the fort of the Tunica village, about thirty leagues (90 miles) from the river. He stayed with his troops and the Tunicas for several years. When he left four years later in 1734, he reported to his commander Maurepas that a detachment of soldiers still resided with the Tunicas.

A report written on December 20, 1737, stated that the Tunicas had killed all the French soldiers and settlers at Natchez. A small French garrison, all that was left among the Tunicas, had moved to Pointe Coupee only seven leagues (21 miles) away. Before they left, the French demolished the fort, leaving the Tunicas with no protection if they decided to return later.

Fort Tunica was built approximately eighteen leagues (54 miles) from Natchez on the east banks of the Mississippi River in present-day Mississippi.

It was at the south end of the Portage of the Cross, now West Feliciana Parish, near the end of the Old River. Nothing remains of the fort except the legend of the massacre and the noises that come from the wooded area nearby. Anyone who goes to the end of Old River might hear the war chants and cries of terror and pain. These sounds are echoes from the past, and they are as frightening today as they were the first time they were heard.

26

FORT DESPERATE/PORT HUDSON

Marching men have been seen several times at the Port Hudson State Historic site. Thurman has asked himself many times if the men were reenactors or ghosts as he watched Confederate-clad men marching back and forth near the Fort Desperate breastworks at the historic overlook. He stood at the overlook site and watched, intent on the uniforms and the expressions on the soldiers' faces. Then he noticed bloodstains on their pants and blood on their shirts and coats. The column of soldiers turned and marched back toward him. He saw more blood, and from where he stood, he saw bandages on their heads, arms, and legs covered in blood. Curiosity got the better of him, and he stepped from the overlook and walked closer to what he thought were reenactors. He wanted to ask them some questions. How did they become reenactors? Why were they dressed as wounded soldiers? The closer he came to the marching men, the more he noticed a putrid odor. Soon he wrinkled his nostrils at the stench of death and bloodied wounds. He hurried away from the marching soldiers and stood waiting and wondering what was going on.

Thurman left the vicinity of the overlook and went straight to the museum, where he hoped he could find someone else who knew about the men in the field. As he told Tom about the men he'd seen and their condition, Tom nodded. He explained to Thurman that those men were seen on occasion, but that there was nothing to be done for them. They were the ghosts of the men who died at Fort Desperate. He told Thurman about the first time he'd seen the men.

That day there were reenactors on the field, and they had also reported the men marching with bandages. They had been called into camp, but they continued to march. Tom said they all thought the men were just reenactors practicing for the next day's events. The men never did come into camp or to the overlook nearby. As Tom and the others watched, the soldiers marched back and forth as if putting on a demonstration. As darkness fell across the park, Tom and the others who watched with him saw the soldiers vanish into the darkness of the night. The soldiers' voices began to ring out loud and clear. Tom and the others waited for the soldiers to stop in at the campfire. The marching group's voices faded into the darkness and were quiet until the next morning. At dawn, the same men were back in the field marching, and were observed by the group with Tom who had stayed around to see if the soldier apparitions would return.

Ever watchful for accuracy in the reenactors, Tom had taken note of the ghostly marching unit on the grounds. They were doing extremely well. He walked to the area where the soldiers were practicing their maneuvers. When Tom came closer to the soldiers, they strategically moved away. As they neared the creek behind the Fort Desperate breastworks, the soldiers disappeared into the misty nothingness of yesteryear.

Tom and his friends went through the next day teaching tourists the history of what has sometimes been called the longest siege of the Civil War.

Walking along the six miles around the Port Hudson site, visitors will be transported to the days of death and destruction of the Civil War. The Confederacy needed to keep supplies flowing to their troops from the Mississippi, and the north needed to split the Confederacy. In order to accomplish either of these objectives, both sides had to control the river. Without control of Port Hudson, the river was useless to both sides.

New Orleans fell to the Union in April of 1862, thus causing Confederate control of the Mississippi to be in danger. With the bluffs near Vicksburg, Mississippi, heavily guarded, the Confederates felt the need to fortify the mouth of the Red River as well. The Red River soon became the Rebel's main route for receiving supplies from Texas.

Port Hudson on the bluffs represented a great site for the new batteries. The severe bend of the river made it too difficult for Union warships to maneuver. Only after their defeat at the Battle of Baton Rouge, the Confederates marched to Port Hudson, intent to occupy the area. They arrived August 15, 1862. In the months that followed, the soldiers worked and built four-and-one-half miles of earthworks and a series of batteries to protect the area.

With approximately eighty-six hundred troops under his command, Confederate Major General Franklin Gardner encountered about thirty thousand Union troops led by Major General Nathaniel P. Banks on May 23, 1863. The Confederates defended four-and-a-half miles of earthworks along Port Hudson with courage and bravery.

Filled with determination, some 292 officers and men worked under Colonel Benjamin W. Johnson day and night, under fire, to construct the breastworks of Fort Desperate, about three-quarters of a mile long. The Confederates held the Union soldiers off. The natural terrain of Fort Desperate played a huge role in the Rebels soldiers' strength and stamina against such odds. The Confederate soldiers fought from within the stronghold of the fort, rarely ever more than one hundred and fifty yards from any point within their works.

The forty-eight-day siege of Port Hudson ended, and the terms of surrender were negotiated on July 9, 1863, at which time the Yankee soldiers entered Port Hudson. At the end of the battle of Port Hudson, often referred to as the longest and bloodiest battle in American military history, the site was used as a recruiting station for African-American troops. Two of these African-American regiments were used in the Port Hudson siege on an experimental basis. The use of these regiments at Port Hudson and the Union victory were highly acclaimed in Northern newspapers. The African-American garrison was kept at Port Hudson until the summer of 1866.

The U. S. Department of the Interior proclaimed Port Hudson with Fort Desperate together a national historic landmark in 1974. Port Hudson is located on U.S. Highway 61 in East Feliciana Parish. It is about twenty-five minutes north of Baton Rouge and only ten minutes south of historic St. Francisville.

The historic site hosts Living History Days several times a year. Visitors to Port Hudson come from all across America to see the authentically dressed interpreters demonstrate the Civil War weapons and equipment. While visitors watch these demonstrations, it is likely they will see the ghostly soldiers practicing on the field with the reenactors. A closer look may be called for to see the soldiers from another realm.

27

FORT SAN CARLOS

Two students at the Louisiana State University in Baton Rouge made a habit of taking a Saturday picnic near the mounds of the Native Americans, located on the university's campus. On one particular weekend, things were different when Tamra arrived to await her friend. As she made her way to the northwestern corner of the campus, she stopped abruptly, hearing strange noises. Yelling and screaming echoed from a distance. The closer she came to the ceremonial centers, the more frightened she became, but she couldn't stop. She felt drawn to the mounds. The scenes that greeted her still live in her mind.

One group of men with muskets shot at another group. Fire erupted from the ends of the rifles they aimed. The loud booms that resounded across the campus caused Tamra to jump and squeal in terror. As she rounded the corner, she witnessed the first death of the conflict. A ghost-like figure was running into a group of men shooting at him. The spectral figure dodged this way and that as he ran across the campus. The man stopped in mid-stride after a whistling sound and a loud thud resounded through the air. For a moment the man stood still, his mouth gaping open. Slowly he sank to the ground. Tamra noticed blood staining the uniform over his heart. Judging from the uniform of the man who fell, he was an officer. Just seconds after he wilted to the ground, a man kneeling over him was shot in the heart. Blood covered his shirt front as he fell across the first man. Tamra heard her own scream mingle with the others around her. As she watched the dead men, the others at the mound disappeared into a misty fog that silently enveloped the area.

Astonished at the scene she'd witnessed, she shivered in the wet rainy conditions, a sudden weather change. Sitting hard on the ground near the two felled men, she watched them as they too disappeared into the fog. Two men had been killed, but there were no killers; the bodies of those who were killed had disappeared. Half an hour later, she still sat near the mounds. The sun shone brightly on her and the rest of the campus. When her friend finally showed up for their picnic, Tamra was still confused and dazed. She allowed her friend to take her back to the dorm, and she filled her in on the happenings of the morning.

Later in the evening, the two girls went for a walk to clear their minds. Tamra said they couldn't stay away from the mound. As they reached the corner of the university campus, they halted abruptly. Lying on the ground in front of them were two men, blood seeping into the ground and from under their bodies. Tamra reached to touch them, but as she did, they turned into dust. The girls stood watching a couple of minutes, not able to believe what they had witnessed.

Tamra says that as she stood at the place for only a few moments her feet began to get freezing cold. The coldness spread up her legs until her knees became stiff and she fell to the ground. Her friend helped her to her feet, and then they left the mounds quickly. Tamra says she looked back and saw a long stick buried in the ground, coated with blood. She never returned to the mounds as long as she attended the university.

Two ancient mounds created by the Native Americans stand on the northwest corner of Louisiana State University. These mounds were used as base camps for the Indians while they were hunting and gathering food. The Indians used the mounds as ceremonial centers as well. The mounds represented different tribes. The Houmas tribes lived to the north of the "red stick" and the Bayogoulas to the south. The "red stick" was a boundary marker. The Indians had buried a stick in the ground and covered it in animal blood. The French explorers who found the stick and the mounds in 1699 called the area "red stick"—*baton rouge*—from which the town gets its name.

Around 1718, the French actually settled the area later known as Fort San Carlos. They left the area by 1727. Much later, in 1763, the British established the first military outpost on the same site where the French first settled, Fort Richmond. Many present-day citizens of Baton Rouge can trace their origins to the first commander of the fort, Captain George Johnstone.

On September 21, 1779, after an eight-day siege, the British surrendered under heavy bombardment by Spanish guns. Lieutenant Colonel Alexander Dickson gave over possession of Fort San Carlos to Louisiana

Governor Bernardo de Galvez, who then gave command of Fort San Carlos to Captain Pedro Favrot.

Galvez's description of Fort San Carlos in a report to the French officials shows a fort made of dirt in the same area as the ancient mounds. It consisted of a ditch eighteen feet wide and nine feet high and sloping. It had a parapet and chevaux-de-frise (spikes along the top of the wall). The fort was armed with thirteen large-caliber cannons. Favrot kept up repairs on Fort San Carlos during his two years of service. The fort fell to disrepair from then until the early 1790s when Governor Carondelet came along. Carondelet made a deal with William Dunbar for timber to repair the fort. Dunbar furnished the timber for repairs in 1787, but apparently only part of the fort was repaired.

Later in 1799, a company of men was sent into the swamps to retrieve pickets for the fort. In July of the same year, three carts and eleven oxen were sold at auction after being used at Fort San Carlos. These items were sold to recoup at least some of the money spent on the fort. There was very little work done despite the request for funds to improve the state of the fort.

Dr. John Sibley reported to his American superiors that there were thirty different-sized cannons mounted at the fort. This number varied from the reports given upon the purchase of the territory of Louisiana.

From 1802 until September 1810, a garrison of fifty American soldiers under Spanish rule was stationed at Fort San Carlos. On the night of September 22, 1810, troops of the West Florida Convention revolted against the Spanish and seized the fort. Two men were killed that night, Spanish Commander Lieutenant Louis Grandpre and one of his men. In December of 1810, the Republic of West Florida turned the fort over to the United States. At this time, the Americans deemed the fort of little value.

During the War of 1812, a New Orleans engineer was employed to prepare a plan of the Fort of Baton Rogue/Fort San Carlos. He proposed a renovation, but nothing indicates that the rebuilding of the fort ever took place. The Baton Rouge Pentagon Barracks were built on top of the old fort and Native American mounds between 1819 and 1824. Apparently dirt from the fort parapets filled the ravines on the post grounds.

The remains of the mounds and the fort can be found at 330 Thomas Boyd Hall in Baton Rouge, Louisiana.

Students of the University of Louisiana see many things and study many more. Tamra's report of what she and her friend saw has been the only one in recent years. The battle may be fought only a few times or any time someone with an open mind visits the university.

28

BATON ROUGE ARSENAL

On a cool rainy day, three young men attending Louisiana State University took books from the main library to the Old Arsenal for storage. Horsing around, they knocked some books from a self. The building echoed the thudding sounds long after the books were picked up.

They looked at one another and smiled. Then they started making fun noises to hear the echoes. They didn't laugh much after that. A shotgun blast resounded through the old building. They thought someone was shooting outside and were frightened.

Hank huddled under one of the shelves, and the other boys had to coax him out.

Gunfire, loud and clear, became masked in cries for help. The boys eased outside. Nothing unusual was taking place. There were no odd noises, nothing out of the ordinary.

John told the other boys he wasn't scared of anything. He just hoped that whoever was shooting had gone away.

Hank has gone back several times after that one incident, and the noises are still there. He's asked questions and found out they weren't the only ones to hear the guns firing and the other battle sounds.

Jason didn't believe in spirits or anything he couldn't see until the incident at the arsenal. He had seen things he hadn't told anyone else about. That's why he never went to the Old Arsenal alone. He had worked at the old building for a while. He did research on the Arsenal, and some nights he had to stay at the building to read. One night he had been reading about the Old Arsenal. It had at one time been called Fort Richmond in the 1760s, and he believes that the ghost of Governor Bernardo de Galvez still visits the Old Baton Rouge Arsenal.

John and Hank questioned Jason as to why he believed what he did about the old governor, Galvez. He told them of the last night he stayed over to research. He sat at one of the tables reading, and a gaunt man came up to the table and stood glaring at him. His eyes were glowing red and yellow, like flames of a fire. The man didn't look like anyone Jason knew, and he never spoke a word. Jason asked what he wanted, and the man motioned for him to leave. The apparition jerked his thumb toward the door, his face full of dislike. Jason refused, and the man became agitated. He wasn't dressed in modern clothes. He looked as if he were in costume. When Jason continued to refuse to leave the building, the man got furious and turned red in the face. His eyes were what finally convinced Jason to leave. The spirit's eyes once again turned red and glassy, as if they were on fire. Jason didn't waste any more time. He left the arsenal and has not returned alone or at night. Jason believes that it is Galvez who roams the Old Baton Rouge Arsenal at night.

The Old Baton Rouge Arsenal standing today is probably the third building that has gone up since it was originally Fort Richmond in the 1760s. The British defenses failed to withstand the Spanish governor Bernardo de Galvez's attack in 1779 when he captured Baton Rouge. After taking over the fortification, Galvez expanded everything and paid special attention to the powder magazine. When the French took over in 1800, there was a brief restoration of the whole fort before 1803, when the United States purchased the Louisiana Territory. By 1812, Louisiana had become the eighteenth state of the union, and the U. S. army had taken over the fort.

Work began again on the fort, first at the Pentagon Barracks and then to build a new powder magazine. The magazine was soon declared too small, and authorities thought it was located too close to the barracks. Then the present-day arsenal was constructed.

In the late 1830s, Baton Rouge was a major staging area for the troops who fought in the Mexican War. It housed such distinguished officers as General Zachary Taylor, Robert E. Lee, Jefferson Davis, William T. Sherman, George B. McClellan, P. G. T. Beauregard, and Ulysses S. Grant.

On January 26, 1861, Louisiana seceded from the Union. At this time, Thomas Moore, then governor, acted quickly and seized control of the arsenal. Louisiana joined the Confederate States of America and needed weapons and ammunition. The powder magazine at Baton Rouge was full of necessities that were rushed to the troops of the Southern units in battle.

In May 1862, the Union troops recaptured Louisiana's capital city. Later, U. S. Marines and army troops controlled Fort Richmond and the Old Arsenal with its large powder magazine. Confederate soldiers under the direction of General John C. Breckenridge tried to remove the Union troops from the fortification and drive them into the Mississippi River. They failed.

Several years after the Civil War, jurisdiction of the Arsenal was transferred from the Ordnance Corps to the Quartermaster's Department. The munitions and equipment stored at the Arsenal were sent to Rock Island, Illinois. In 1884, the post that once protected Baton Rouge came under the control of the U. S. Department of the Interior. Later, in 1886, the entire property was given back to the Louisiana State University. The powder magazine was used as storage for the state library and at one time, as a barn.

Huey P. Long, governor of Louisiana, developed a grand plan for a new capital in Baton Rouge, and the Old Arsenal was to lose its life and be demolished. However, he was dissuaded by a group of citizens led by Edward McIllhenny, and left the powder magazine intact. Later the Manchac Chapter of the Daughters of the Revolution thwarted another similar threat to the Old Arsenal. Since that time, the arsenal has served the state police and the National Guard, and, in more recent years, it has been reincarnated as a wonderful museum filled with memorabilia of the Old South and a way of life long dead. There are displays of Civil War uniforms and weaponry as well. Like a sentinel of the past, the powder magazine reminds the citizens of Louisiana of their rich heritage.

The Old Baton Rouge Arsenal is located in Baton Rouge on State Capital Drive right next to the State Capitol building.

Visiting the Old Arsenal museum is a wonderful experience. Close scrutiny of the displays may possibly bring an even more wonderful experience if the spirit of Governor Galvez happens to be at the Arsenal. He has been known to be in the building at night.

V

Greater New Orleans

Camp Moore

Fort Macomb

Fort Pike

Fort Massachusetts

Fort Livingston

Fort Proctor/ Fort Beauregard

Fort Jackson

Fort St. John

Fort Petite Coquilles

Fort St. Philip

Camp Parapet

Fort De La Boulaye

29

CAMP MOORE

Closed to the public for several years, Camp Moore has many visitors today. Some of the visitors are even from the past. One visitor is a beautiful woman dressed in white. Mrs. E. Beachbard has been seen with her old-fashioned camera on the Camp Moore grounds, where she takes pictures of other visitors and the soldiers at Camp Moore. One of her subjects, a fellow named Dawson, has a handmade card the lady gave him. He's never received his photo, but the experience of having met the lady apparition was worth the price of the photo, he says.

Dawson went out to the Camp Moore site, now only a cemetery. A woman walked up to him and handed him a card. She seemed so bright and her eyes twinkled. He noticed the large antique camera and tripod set up not too far from where they stood. Fumbling with the card she gave him, he read what was on the paper. He read that she was an ambrotype photographer. Her name was Mrs. E. Beachbard. The longer they talked, the more convinced Dawson was that he needed his picture taken. He allowed her to pose him, and she stood behind the camera. He thought how neat it was for reenactors to stay at the historic site and entertain visitors. As the woman finished taking his photo, he reached into his wallet to pay her for her service.

When she saw the money he handed her, she took it and looked at it intensely. She tossed the money back at him and uttered something about not wanting his kind of money. Her expression changed instantly. She turned on her heel and stalked back to her camera. She packed it and began to leave. He stood, shocked at her attitude, and watched her weave in and out of the headstones. As she walked, she vanished among the stones.

Dawson is not the only person to see the spirit of Mrs. Beachbard. One woman says she took a picture of Mrs. Beachbard taking photos of soldiers and their families. The lady who took the picture was ecstatic when she developed her film. The pictures showed only misty shadows of the people she photographed. The woman often visits Camp Moore, hoping to see Mrs. Beachbard again.

Jean visited Camp Moore on a whim while in Louisiana. She took photos of the headstones at the Confederate cemetery. She was always taking pictures at cemeteries, looking for spirits.

Late in the afternoon, just before dusk, Jean saw a woman taking photos with a large antique camera on a tripod. She began snapping her own pictures of the woman in the white dress. When she looked through the viewfinder, Jean saw that the woman was taking photos of a soldier. They must be reenactors, she thought. The period clothing the two wore looked authentic. Jean watched them for a few minutes and then turned to take more photos of the area. When she looked back where the two people had been standing, they had disappeared. This gave Jean the idea that the two were apparitions and she was excited about processing the photos she had taken. Her photos proved she was right, and she couldn't wait to return to Camp Moore. She returned to the Camp Moore site many times to see if she could contact the woman in white. She knew that her ghost-hunting friends would be interested in Camp Moore and Mrs. Beachbeard as well.

Visitors have often heard horrible screams piercing the air from the direction of the railroad tracks behind the camp site. The sound of running feet can also be heard shortly afterward, then more shrieks of pain. Wails are heard through the chaos. Men's voices are heard, shouting orders. Sobs from a broken-hearted woman break through the turmoil. Finally silence prevails, and then only the normal sounds of everyday life

Another visitor to Camp Moore told of seeing an officer, probably a general, from the look of his uniform. The officer walked around saluting as someone passed him. He stood at attention at a particular point, and then he suddenly fell to the ground. The fallen soldier soon faded into the turf of the Camp Moore Cemetery.

Approximately seventy-five miles from New Orleans sits Camp Moore and the cemetery where several hundred men are buried. The camp site, between New Orleans and Lake Pontchartrain, was named for Governor Thomas Overton Moore. A walkway was built to the camp, only a half-mile long from Camp Moore to Tangipahoa.

Most of the volunteers from Louisiana gathered at Camp Moore when the call went out for men to fight the Civil War. The men were organized into regiments, later to be trained for war. Some of the companies were funded by the military, while others were privately funded. Twenty-eight

Thomas Overton Moore was the governor of Louisiana for a short time during the Civil War. His portrait hangs at the Historic Mansfield Battlefield Museum.

volunteer companies were furnished their weapons by the military. These weapons and ammunition were taken from the Union forces that had held Baton Rouge hostage. A total of 1,765 men who enlisted in the Confederate army were gathered at Camp Moore. The men split into companies ranging in size from thirty to one hundred twenty men. These companies garrisoned the forts of the Confederate states. Governor Moore released state troops to go into Confederate service. This cleared the way for individual citizens also to volunteer their services.

On April 8, 1861, a call came from Confederate president Jefferson Davis. He asked for another three thousand troops. After the Fort Sumter incident, he asked for another five thousand volunteers. These troops, sent to New Orleans to protect the city, gathered at the Metairie Racecourse. The course was then used for the three thousand men who had to be turned into fighting men instead of farmers. This training place, Camp Walker, wasn't very good for training purposes. There was a lack of clean water, the mosquitoes swarmed the men, and the marshy soil left much to be desired for marching and training.

Two men from the surrounding area, Henry Forno and James Wing-field, were sent into the woods to find a suitable place for another camp. Once they settled on an area, troops were sent to clear the woods and brush away, and Camp Moore was born.

With the camp site cleared, General Elisha Tracy began transferring his troops from Camp Walker to Camp Moore. Only the 3rd Regiment of Louisiana volunteers was left at the old camp. The regiment completed its training and was sent to other venues of the war.

Camp Moore had abundant water, clear and clean enough for drinking. Because of the trees around the camp, there was plenty of shade and there were hardly any mosquitoes. The soil was well drained and held up well when rain fell. Soldiers came from all over the state by railway, boat, and foot to reach the camp.

Once at the fort, the volunteers had to choose their leaders. This brought about lots of campaigning and political speeches from those who wanted to serve as the leaders of the men. After forming a regiment, the men elected their colonels, lieutenant colonels, and the majors.

Camp Moore consisted of a large commissary and a quartermaster's storehouse. These were located along the railroad tracks for taking supplies to the stores more easily. Also at Camp Moore were a coffee house, a grocery store, several suttlers, soda and refreshment shops, shanty restaurants, a butcher shop, the camping grounds, a large parade ground, and a burial ground. One other establishment was Mrs. E. Beachbard's ambrotype salon, or photographer's shop. Her original shop was in New Orleans, but she saw an opportunity at Camp Moore and took advantage of it.

Three days after the camp was set up, the first casualty took place. A young enlisted member of Wheat's Battalion died in an accident with a rail-car on May 16, 1861. Several epidemics of measles caused many deaths of the men at Camp Moore, as well as the death of Mrs. Beachbard on November 22, 1861.

When the Union forces arrived in New Orleans, Major General Mansfield Lovell ordered all troops to Camp Moore from where they were dispersed in other areas of the war. Eventually the militia was sent home, back to New Orleans. Camp Moore remained a camp for troop instruction of Louisiana conscripts for some time. The camp also served as a prisoner-of-war camp under the command of General Tracy. Upon Tracy's sudden death late in 1862, General Ruggles came to Camp Moore with one thousand men under his command.

In both 1863 and 1864, Camp Moore was raided several times. On the last raid, Union forces destroyed a large amount of stored clothing, a tannery, tanned hides, and parts of other structures in the camp. The Federals captured the garrison flag and ran off or killed a herd of cattle that was to be sent to the Confederate soldiers in the field. Later in 1864, General Davidson of the Union army came through Tangipahoa with about five thousand men. Camp Moore was ordered burned. All the outbuildings were destroyed. One soldier wrote home that the Union men even burned the wooden headboards in the cemetery. Camp Moore was finished in its duty to the Confederate army. For the next thirty years, Camp Moore was vacant of life.

In 1892, the United Confederate Veterans Camp Number 60 was established in Tangipahoa. The sole purpose of the group was to care for the graves at the Camp Moore Cemetery.

Later, the United Daughters of the Confederacy received the donation of a two-acre tract of land containing the cemetery. An appropriation of funds to build a wall or fence around the cemetery was voted in 1904 by the Louisiana Legislature. A monument was dedicated in the cemetery in 1907. Another tract of land was procured for a museum built with state funds and dedicated in May 1965 as a state commemorative area.

Governor Edwards closed the site at Camp Moore and other commemorative areas throughout the state in 1985. There was a lack of funds to keep these areas open at the time. The site at Camp Moore stayed closed until 1993, when a nonprofit entity took over the care of the historical site.

The museum at Camp Moore has displays of Confederate memorabilia depicting life as it was at the camp. There is also the monument at Camp Moore, and the cemetery is open to the public. Camp Moore's museum is open from ten in the morning until three in the afternoon, Tuesday through Saturday. It is located along Highway 51, a half-mile from Tangipahoa. Visitors who travel to Camp Moore may be lucky enough to be approached by a lady photographer dressed in period clothes. The woman in white isn't out to steal a soul, but the visitor might not get the photos the woman takes. She wants only Confederate money for her work.

30

FORT MACOMB

When Jason stopped in a nearby marina and asked if there was any way he could see Fort Macomb up close, he was taken on a private tour of the ruins. The architecture is an exact replica of its sister fort, Fort Pike. Jason says staying at the fort for very long isn't safe because of the spirits that linger there. He felt a distinct presence at the fort. That presence was not a friendly one. As he walked from one part of the fort to another, he felt he was being carefully watched. Not only did he find several cold spots, but he also felt an oppression he'd never felt before.

Standing to look through a slit in the wall, he said he felt a hand on his shoulder. When he turned to see who was behind him, there was no one. Once he felt a hand on his back, and he was shoved hard. He almost fell to his knees but caught his balance quickly. Jason feels that he was not wanted at the ruins. He hasn't figured out why the spirits don't want him at the fort, but he isn't interested in finding out now, either. He thinks that some of the soldiers who manned the fort in the past are still there, guarding Lake Pontchartrain.

At one point when he stopped to take pictures, Jason heard a deep voice whispering to him that he must leave at once. Not one to be frightened easily, Jason continued shooting photos for several minutes. He changed film. While he had his camera open, something or someone began tugging on the camera. After starting the new film in the camera, he clicked frame after frame in the direction the tugging had come from, and a strange gurgling noise began growing louder and louder. The more pictures he snapped, the louder the noise became. He took a few more shots and left quickly. The tour guide had gone to wait in the boat.

Jason says he isn't easily frightened by much at historical places. He has seen and dealt with spirits before, but this one frightened him. He recommends that visitors go to the marina and take their pictures from afar. Jason says none of the pictures he took developed properly. Most of the photos were totally black. He went back later in the year, and the new photos turned out the have orbs and misty forms on the pictures. Fort Macomb is an old fort with many memories and spirits, but Jason refuses to visit it again.

Because of Corsairs who attacked Spanish vessels using the route via Mobile and Pensacola to Bayou St. John behind New Orleans, Fort Chef Menteur was established. Governor Carondelet recommended that the fort be erected. In 1792 the fort had at least four cannons to protect its walls and the soldiers who lived there.

General Andrew Jackson feared the British would use shoal boats on the south side of Bayou Sauvage and attack New Orleans. At this point he garrisoned the fort with free Negroes when he placed a battery at the site of the old Fort Chef Menteur in 1814. After the completion of the batteries at the junction of the bayou and the pass, the Fortifications Board decided there was a need for another fort. Sources indicate that it took three years to build the fort. The actual work did not start on the fort until 1822. Not until January of 1828 was the fort finished and manned. At this time, reports from the fort began to reach General Jackson. However, another report dated October 31, 1827, lists Captain Samuel Spotts as commander of two other officers and thirty-seven enlisted men of the 4th Artillery.

Between 1828 and 1835, there were many other commanders and units posted at the new fort, named Fort Wood during this time. The cost of the fort to the War Department was approximately $311,000 because of its brick construction. Passageways throughout the inside of the fort were also built of brick and offered the double protection of solid walls. The outer walls sported square holes for rifles and placements for the larger cannons. The outside perimeter of the fort was built in a triangular arc. The sides of the fort's walls were arched slightly instead of being built straight. The fort's outside walls had a large bastion at the two land junctions and a demi-bastion at the curved waterfront along the moat. It measured 308 yards at the parapets. The foundation of the fort was made of shells, logs, and cross timbers. At some point in these years, the fort's name was changed again to Fort Macomb. The manpower of the fort remained short until just before the Civil War.

Confederate Governor T. O. Moore seized all federal installations in Louisiana in 1861. When the governor ordered the seizures on January 23, 1861, Captain Clinch did as he was commanded and took control of Fort Macomb. Four days later, he manned the fort with forty Confederate troops. A month later, the commanding officer was told to remove the cannons from Fort Macomb and transport them to another fort in the area. Macomb was deemed to be of little help to the cause of the war at the time, while other fortress locations were obviously more important.

When the Americans first chose the site for Fort Macomb, there was no title to be found for the land. Bartholomew Lafon, Jean Lafitte's right-hand man, claimed he was the owner of the property. He said he had bought the property from Louis Decouet in 1801. There were others who laid claim to the property as well. The land was finally confirmed to Lafon by the U. S. Land Commissioners.

The land passed from hand to hand through heirs until August 11, 1911, when just over sixteen acres were sold to the Motor League of Louisiana. On March 27, 1939, the Motor League deeded the 16.03 acres of Fort Macomb to the State Parks Commission of Louisiana. Twelve hundred yards of the outside salients of Fort Macomb were withdrawn from the public domain in February of 1942 and reserved for military purposes. By executive order, the state gave up jurisdiction of the land.

Later, in 1966, the State Parks Commission leased the 16.03 acres to the Fort Macomb Development Corporation. There were some preservationists who were upset with public officials over this, and in 1981, state officials came up with a way to preserve the old fort site. They purchased the Fort Macomb area and took immediate possession. The state began to try to fix the maintenance problems of the site.

A fire destroyed the barracks, and a portion of the moat is now used by a local marina. Visitors can get a glimpse of the fortress from the marina. Fort Macomb lies about one hundred and fifty yards to the west of Chef Menteur Bridge on the southwest bank of the winding waterway joining Lake Pontchartrain, Lake Borgue, and the Gulf of Mexico between Highway 90 and the Louisville and Nashville Railroad.

If visitors want to go across the moat to see Fort Macomb up close, they should be sure to go on the buddy system. Some of the spirits left behind at the fort do not appreciate visitors. Jason says they sure don't like photographers and their cameras.

31

FORT PIKE

Walking through the passageway of Fort Pike, visitors have been confronted with eerie sounds and a feeling of being watched. When Jackie walked down the dungeon-like paths, she heard men whispering, but there was no one else in this part of the fort with her. One voice she remembered distinctly was gravelly sounding. It spoke in low grumbling tones that frightened her. Once the voices quieted, she saw a patch of light shining on the brick walls. The patch of light moved here and there. She searched for the source of the light, but found nothing. It amazed her that the light was there, moving around like a flashlight, but there was no flashlight in the tunnel or anything else to reflect light.

Maybe her friends were playing tricks on her, but she didn't see any signs of anyone else. She had left her friends at another part of the fort. Suddenly she felt a cold chill spread over her body. Then she felt a large hand grab her shoulder and squeeze gently. She looked around, and standing directly behind her was a large ghost-like man. His hair was jet black and his eyes were the same. Their gazes met. Jackie swallowed hard and stammered a bit before demanding that he let go of her shoulder. She asked to know just exactly who he thought he was and what he wanted from her.

The spirit grinned at her and motioned for her to move toward the end of the passageway. She walked slowly at first. She didn't really feel scared any longer, so she allowed herself to be escorted out of the passages by the spirit.

Once out in the sunlight, Jackie felt the presence disappear from behind her. She met her friends and told them what had happened. She listened to their stories of what happened to them. Her friends thought they saw the cannon being moved and aimed out to sea. They said there had been a huge man standing at the cannon, moving it.

Fort Pike guarded New Orleans in the past and perhaps still does. However, Jackie believes the cannons were moved by a black soldier. She saw a man standing near the gunnery placement after she came out of the passages. The voice she heard earlier in her visit had been giving orders to "drill until the use of the cannon becomes commonplace."

As Jackie and her friends were leaving, they say they heard a loud Rebel yell. The four women reached their vehicle and sat listening for a few moments before driving away from Fort Pike's historic site.

Fort Pike, like several others, was designed by Simon Bernard, a French engineer. He was hired by the U. S. government to design the coastal series of forts. Fort Pike was built between 1819 and 1826. It is located at the Rigolets between Lake Pontchartrain and the Gulf of Mexico. New Orleans is not far from the fort. The swamplands around the fort afforded many challenges to the builders. The worst problem the builders had was in building a strong foundation. The foundation had to be created from the few resources available from the swamps in the area. The builders sank several layers of cypress log "rafts" into the muddy swamps. They were then covered with a layer of sea shells to create a base for the fort supports. Since logs do not rot unless exposed to the wetting and drying process, this foundation has held up rather well.

The fort was built over the old site of "Petites Coquilles," French for "Little Shells." This was also the name of the island. The first building of a fort was in 1793 under the rule of Governor Carondelet. The present construction was done by Americans who retained the Old World feudal atmosphere, apparent in the curved semicircular moat, dungeon-like passageways, and the barbette tier of gunnery placements on the brick ramparts. One of the neatest features of the fort is the casement design. There is a narrow tunnel leading to the open area where the cannons were mounted in place. Fort Pike and its sister fort, Fort McComb, the only two forts with this type of design, are connected by a narrow parkway. Other Louisiana coastal forts designed by Bernard were constructed to be more like American designs, with casements open at the back.

After the fort was finished, Fort Pike was manned irregularly through the years. Used as a staging area in the 1830s during the Seminole Wars, Fort Pike was where troops gathered before marching to Florida. The fort was also used as a collection station for the Seminole prisoners as well as their black slaves. Hundreds of prisoners were taken and then transported to Oklahoma to the reservations.

Some ten or so years later, Fort Pike was used in much the same manner during the Mexican Wars. Soldiers stopped in at Fort Pike as they were bound for Texas and Mexico. The fort had been semi-abandoned between the Mexican War and the Civil War. Only one sergeant took care of the fort between the two wars. A single ordnance sergeant was in command of Fort Pike in 1861 when Louisiana seceded from the Union and took over Fort Pike without a single shot being fired.

After the capture of New Orleans by Union troops, Fort Pike once again fell into the hands of the Union. The Confederates didn't give up easily; they destroyed the cannons and set fire to the wooden structures behind the fort walls. Union forces took control and used Fort Pike for training purposes for colored troops. The army trained freed slaves in the use of heavy artillery. They were sent into battle in other areas of the country. Not one cannon was ever fired in battle from Fort Pike.

Once thought to be impregnable, Fort Pike became useless when someone developed artillery with higher velocity and larger caliber guns. After Fort Sumter was destroyed by these new weapons, Fort Pike was deemed obsolete. In its day, the fort was thought to be essential for the protection of a growing nation.

From 1871 until 1890, when it was abandoned by the army, an ordnance soldier remained in control of the fort. The state of Louisiana took over the care of Fort Pike when it became a commemorative area. Today Fort Pike is behind a fence. The museum opened in the fall of 1970. In the museum there are exhibits of Confederate uniforms. Also displayed were dress and battle orders for the War of 1812 to the Civil War. A collection of newspapers of the 1860s is also on display. The fort was put on the National Register of Historic places in 1972.

The Fort Pike historic site is off U.S. Highway 90 about 23 miles east of downtown New Orleans. It is also accessible from I-10 off Louisiana State Highway 11 south and then U.S. Highway 90. Visitors to the fort enjoy picnics and walk through the displays of uniforms and other memorabilia in the museum. They walk through the arched casements or stand lookout over the Rigolets as soldiers once did or maybe still do. If visitors look close enough and keep an open mind, they might be able to see some of the spirits who remain at Fort Pike. These spirits may decide to show themselves either on the grounds or in the casements and passageways of the fort. When visitors leave Fort Pike, the Rebel yell might he heard.

32

FORT MASSACHUSETTS

A cold wet wind blew from the Gulf side of Ship Island. Visitors to the ruins of Fort Massachusetts scrambled for cover from the approaching storm. The charter boat came shortly afterward. As the tourists began loading onto the craft, Shane looked back beyond the museum. Men in blue uniforms ran here and there, just ahead of a menacing storm cloud.

Shane peered at the people on the boat; most of them were sitting quietly, and some talked to their neighbors. No one else had seen the soldiers or the clouds rolling in from the sea side of the island. He turned back to the scene. There were soldiers wet, broken, and strewn across the grounds of the fort. Some of the bodies lay still in death while others moaned and cried in pain. He rubbed his eyes, but the scene continued. A pounding rain poured down upon the fort, but no more than a sprinkle hit the charter boat and its passengers.

Later in the week, Shane made the trek back to Fort Massachusetts, curious to see if the same scene would replay. He stayed about a half-hour, waiting to catch another glimpse of the soldiers. His wait was finally rewarded. The same scene started to unfold before his eyes. The blue uniformed men ran from the cloud, stumbling and falling over one another. When he turned away from the macabre scene and looked back, nothing but fog could be seen covering the island. Afterward, Shane left and has made only one more trip to Ship Island.

The last time he visited Ship Island and Fort Massachusetts, he talked to a man who looked like a maintenance man. He introduced himself as "Pop." Shane felt a little strange about Pop. He couldn't put a finger on anything in particular. The longer he talked to the old gentleman the more convinced he was that something was wrong. He looked closer at Pop's clothing. It was tattered and torn, probably Civil War period. The garments fit loosely on the old man's shoulders.

Shane gazed into Pop's eyes, which seemed to have measureless depth. Shane could see forever into the man's eyes. Maybe it was nothing to worry about. He was just an old man. Shane explained the strange scene he had witnessed. Pop told him that he must have been seeing things. The only time something like that happened was way back in 1861 when Union soldiers occupied Fort Massachusetts. At least that was the last time he knew of a hurricane damaging the fort. Pop said the hurricanes and the heat caused a lot of the soldiers to lose their minds and die. He told Shane they died from exposure and disease. Shane had thought that Pop didn't look too healthy himself, but the old man seemed to know a lot about the history of the fort. For a moment Shane turned away from the caretaker to look out to sea. When he turned back, Pop had disappeared. No one Shane asked knew about Pop. Shane went home and started doing some research and finally found out about the old man. He was a caretaker at the fort, all right, but in 1866.

Once the War of 1812 was over, the U. S. government figured Ship Island needed more protection. With more protection needed for New Orleans, the War Department planned masonry forts for its coastal defenses. Ship Island was the most important area for the protection of New Orleans. In 1847, the government declared the island a reservation for the military. Nine years later, Congress finally gave permission for construction of a fort on the island. The chosen site was about five hundred yards from the western end of the island.

Construction began on Fort Massachusetts in 1859. The work was mostly done by civilians, while the Army Corps of Engineers supervised the overall construction. As many as one hundred men at a time worked on the fort, including carpenters, blacksmiths, masons, stonecutters, and others. The walls stood from six to eight feet tall by 1861.

After the secession of Mississippi, a group of militia stormed the fort and took possession of it and Ship Island. Before long the militia abandoned everything, and the fort was left empty until the Confederates manned it in June of 1861. After taking over the fort, the Confederate soldiers mounted several cannons. Less than a month later, those cannons were used to protect the fort from invasion by the Union Army. The Union ironclad *Massachusetts* came to Ship Island and was driven away in a twenty-minute exchange of cannon fire. Only a few injuries were incurred during the exchange. Neither side sustained much damage. This fight was the only military engagement in which Fort Massachusetts or Ship Island was involved.

The Confederate soldiers spent the rest of the summer of 1861 strengthening the fortress walls. They used timbers and sandbags to complete this task. Despite all the work they did, the soldiers had to leave the fort and the island behind. The Union forces moved in and took over everything. Ship Island was used by the Union as a staging area during the remainder of the war. The officials from the North needed to capture New Orleans, and Ship Island. Fort Massachusetts was the first step in that direction.

Union forces of approximately eighteen thousand men manned Fort Massachusetts. There were few casualties from war, but the weather wreaked havoc on the Northern soldiers. More than 230 men died as a result of the island's harsh environment. These men were eventually moved from their graves on Ship Island to Chalmette National Cemetery near New Orleans.

With the spring of 1862 came the successful results of the Union's capture of New Orleans. Through the remainder of the war, Union soldiers made good use of Fort Massachusetts and Ship Island. Their ships often weighed anchor at the island for repairs or to take on supplies as well as leave supplies for the soldiers there. While on the island, the Union recruited one of the first all-black regiments to serve in the U. S. Army. The regiment was stationed at Fort Massachusetts for nearly three years. During this time, four buildings were added to the fortress. The ex-slaves built a hospital, barracks, a mess hall, and a bakery. The Army Corps of Engineers also resumed construction on the fort's walls in 1862. Other uses of the fort included serving as a prisoner-of-war camp for captured Confederate soldiers.

The fort was never officially named, and in most reports it was called "Fort on Ship Island." During the war the fort was first called "Massachusetts," probably after the Union ironclad ship. Work continued on the fort until 1866 by the Army Corps of Engineers.

Civilian fort keeper C. H. "Pop" Stone took control of Fort Massachusetts in 1866 after its completion. Stone's duties included maintaining the fort so it would be ready at a moment's notice. When cannons were mounted at the fort, officials sent an ordinance sergeant to take control of the fort's armaments. Before long, the sergeant was given the responsibility for the entire fort, leaving Pop Stone to assume other duties. Nothing was ever heard of Stone after he left Fort Massachusetts. Thus the ordinance sergeant cared for the fort until 1903 when the last man was relieved of duty. Thereafter, only the lighthouse caretaker took care of the fort and the island.

Fort Massachusetts is on the western end of Ship Island about a dozen miles south of Gulfport, Mississippi. Access is possible only by a long, hot boat ride, either your own or a charter boat. Regular runs to the island are made daily. Once visitors on the charter boat reach Ship Island, they are sometimes greeted by an older gentleman in tattered and torn clothes. At times he talks to the visitors, and other times he just waves and smiles. Pop is still taking care of the fort.

33

FORT LIVINGSTON

Jean Lafitte and his band of privateers lived on Grand Terre Island. Lafitte seemed to be at peace with the citizens of New Orleans but at war with the authorities. Even though Fort Livingston was not established in Lafitte's day, the privateer roams the ruins of the old fort. Some visitors to the fort say that they have seen Jean Lafitte at different places among the ruins.

One man who visited the fort said he heard footsteps against the hard earth in the pathways of the fort. He said the footsteps echoed through the labyrinth of pathways. Jerry glimpsed a foggy figure in the fort. The same figure took on the form of Jean Lafitte. Jerry had studied the history of the famous pirate and had become an expert on his biography over the years.

The pirate seems to be a prankster. One visitor was walking along one of the pathways when laughter filled the air from the ceiling to the floor. A little leery, she looked around to see what was going on that was so funny. She found nothing. When she began to resume her walk, she tripped over her untied shoe strings. She knew the strings had been tied before she paused to find out about the laughter. When she tripped, the laughter increased in volume. Embarrassed as she was, she searched for whoever was laughing at her. She found no one in the passages with her. The laughter stopped, and everything became still and very quiet. Further into the tour, she felt as if she was being followed. Looking over her shoulder every few minutes, she never saw anything, but there was a presence there with her. She thinks that Jean Lafitte, the dashing and daring pirate, continues his escapades today at the fort.

Another ghostly apparition has been seen at Fort Livingston. A well-dressed man walks along the fort pathways with paper and quill in hand. He seems to be taking notes. Some say he is Bartholomew Lafon, Lafitte's second-in-command. He was also the designer of Fort Livingston and several other Louisiana forts. Some visitors say they have seen him outside the fort. At those sightings he shakes his head and seems to be disgusted with something he is seeing. Then he rolls out a paper and studies it for a moment, then turns and walks away. He fades into nothing but light in the darkened shadows of the fort's wall.

Darlene has seen the designer several times. Lafon was talking with another spirit on one occasion when she was visiting the fort. She thinks Jean Lafitte and his right-hand man, Lafon, were discussing the plans for Fort Livingston. Perhaps they were discussing a raid or how to avoid the authorities of New Orleans.

On another occasion, battle sounds have been heard, and men in everyday clothing can be seen running here and there. Several are being led away by men in uniform while others fall to the ground, covered in blood. Shortly afterward, they disappear. One visitor thinks the scene is that of the capture of Lafitte and his men by the police officers of New Orleans.

With the British invasion imminent, Fort Livingston was built to defend Barataria Pass and New Orleans. On Grand Terre Island, Fort Livingston should have held back any attacking forces. Jean Lafitte the pirate used the island for his headquarters before the Battle of New Orleans. Fort Livingston was planned long before that infamous battle. However, construction was not started until 1841.

Fort Livingston was one of the nine coastal posts built in Louisiana before the Civil War. On May 31, 1813, a plan was proposed for a battery to be built on Grand Terre Island exactly where Lafitte and his men lived. This battery was proposed by Colonel Ross, who hired Bartholomew Lafon to design the fort. In September 1814, Colonel Ross and Commander Daniel T. Patterson destroyed Lafitte's headquarters. Bartholomew Lafon was captured during the attack. Later, it was discovered that Lafon had bought many pieces of property in Louisiana. These properties included some of the Louisiana defense forts. Lafon's plans for the proposed battery on Grand Terre called for the fort to be square and fronted with seven-foot-high parapets and pointed bastions. It would have seven mounted guns.

In 1817, Commander Patterson proposed that the plans for the fort be carried out, and the fort was built. The fort was built the same as two of its sister forts and according to Lafon's plans, with only a few changes. Fort Livingston's plans were changed so that it became a triangular shape with a rounded curtain-like wall that faced Barataria Pass. It had three pointed bastions on the landward sides.

In 1833, the 126.16 acres of land, was surveyed. On January 10, 1834, the property was sold by Etienne de Gruy and his wife, Marie Laure Verloin de Gruy. The jurisdiction of this property was ceded to the United States by the Louisiana legislature on March 10, 1834. It was released by the Louisiana governor later in May of the same year.

Edward Livingston, Andrew Jackson's secretary of state and Jean Lafitte's attorney, was honored to have the fort named after him. Construction on the fort began almost as soon as the deed was transferred. Shortly afterward, on July 11, 1834, building was halted after temporary quarters were built. Construction was stopped because there was no commander for the fort. Later, Captain J. G. Barnard was sent to Fort Livingston to take command and continue with the construction. More temporary buildings, an overseer's quarters, laborers' quarters, kitchens, a carpenter shop, a blacksmith's shop, a wheelbarrow shed, and the master mason's quarters were built. These structures were described as "crude." The shabbily built buildings constructed for the enlisted men saved money for the government. The same plans for the fort called for galleries with millwork on the doors, windows, and fireplace mantels in the officers' quarters, quite unlike the workmanship for the enlisted men's quarters.

In 1840, a wharf was built so that materials could be delivered to the site. Laborers also built an eighteen-hundred-foot railway so that materials could be easily delivered to the site over the muddy terrain.

Fort Livingston was finally erected in a four-sided trapezoid stronghold. It sat inside a moat with outworks on the land side. Bricks were shipped in from out of state, and the shells were removed from Indian mounds in Barataria. Bits of Indian pottery can occasionally be observed in the walls of the fort. Shell was used because it was thought to absorb cannon balls instead of shattering and crumbling into rubble.

At the onset of the Civil War, Fort Livingston was still under construction. Four companies of Confederate soldiers, approximately three hundred strong, were led by General Lovell to man the fort. They brought fifteen cannons with them. On April 27, 1862, the Confederacy took over the fort and held their position until October 26, 1863, when the 16th Regiment Maine Infantry of the Federalists took over.

After the war, the fort was abandoned, and in 1893 a hurricane partially destroyed it. Since the hurricane hit, only the waterfowl, sand crabs, and the spirits of the pirates remain. One lone sugarhouse chimney towers over the wastes of Grand Terre Island, attesting to the past sugarcane fields.

Fort Livingston is on Grand Terre Island and is another of Louisiana's forts that can be reached only by boat. Perhaps Lafitte will captain the boat for visitors to make the trek to Grand Terre Island and Fort Livingston. Maybe other visitors will report seeing Lafitte in a discussion with Lafon.

34

FORT PROCTOR/
FORT BEAUREGARD

Battle sounds from the small island at the mouth of Lake Borgne continue even today.

Reports of soldiers still fighting the Civil War have been made by several folks who live in the vicinity. Harry says he looks out off his front porch and watches strange lights reflect off the water. He isn't sure what is happening out at the old fort, but he doesn't think it is anything good. He's talked to neighbors and they've told him about shadowy shapes inside the walls of the fort. A friend of Harry's has gone out to fish at night, and he's seen eerie reflections emanating from the walls of the fort.

According to Harry, sometimes the fort walls glow like a child's glow-in-the dark toy. At times, the walls look like they are breathing. When he and his friend are out on the lake fishing, the fish never bite up close to the fort, especially when the lights are glowing. One evening they were out on the water, and the walls started glowing. Instead of the usual greenish glow, that night they saw red and yellow against the walls of the fort, as if it was on fire. Curious about what was happening, Harry and his friend went to the fort and left their boat at the bank. They approached the walls of the fort, but there were no lights or flames. They continued to look around. On the parade grounds of the fort they saw the grotesque shadows of fallen men scattered everywhere. The fishermen left the fort in a hurry and agreed they would return the next morning. If the bodies were still there, they'd call the police.

The next morning the men took their boat out to Fort Proctor to see if they had been dreaming. On their way to the fort, the water began to churn. Harry said that something kept rocking his small aluminum craft. He was afraid the boat was going to capsize. He slowed the motor slightly, hoping it would help. It did not. After reaching the fort again, Harry and his

Many Union Soldiers lost their lives on Louisiana soil. Courtesy of Opelousas Chamber of Commerce.

friend went to the place they'd seen the bodies strewn about. There were no bodies in the daylight.

Harry's friend wanted to leave the creepy place. As they walked away from Fort Proctor, Harry looked back, and the bodies were lying there, plain as day. Harry and his friend have not returned to Fort Proctor since.

At one time, swimmers would venture out to the fort to play in the water near the island, but no longer. One of the swimmers claims she was swimming with some friends near the fort when she felt someone pulling on her foot. She thought it might have been one of her friends playing a trick on her. However, her friends were all accounted for when she felt the hand on her foot. Katherine was sure she was going to be drowned. She couldn't get free of whatever it was that had a hold on her. Eventually she kicked her way out of its grasp and swam to where her friends were horsing around. When she told them about her mishap, the boys tried to frighten the girls further by telling them about giant fish. Katherine looked back as they were leaving and saw a man pop his head above water and watch the group. She watched the man rise out of the water and turn to mist. They all warn others not to swim in the waters near the old fort. None of the group has returned to Fort Proctor.

Work began on Fort Proctor, a small square fort with a moat, in 1856 under the supervision of P. G. T. Beauregard. Construction of the fort was very unusual for the era. Structural iron was used to a great extent. A fortress was needed to help guard New Orleans on the western side of Shell Beach. Fort Proctor was only one of the Confederate forts built to guard the Ouachita River. In the waters of Lake Borgne, the fort would help to protect New Orleans.

The fort was never completed because of hurricane damage and the interference of the Civil War. Nevertheless, the Wisconsin 17th Infantry Regiment, which fought thirty-five or more battles during its tenure, brought at least five battles to Fort Proctor on several occasions in 1863.

At one point, Union Lieutenant Colonel Arthur Fremantle of the Coldstream Guard toured the Confederacy and found that Fort Proctor looked far more formidable than he'd expected. In May 1863, the fort was shelled heavily by gunboats on the Ouachita. There were many casualties in the fort. The Confederate soldiers evacuated the fort in September. The first battle the Wisconsin 17th Regiment fought at Fort Proctor/Beauregard began on September 1 and lasted for three days. At that time, the Union troops captured the fort as the Confederate soldiers retreated to fight again another day. That day came sooner than the Union or the Confederacy thought it would. The next day, September 5, the Confederate soldiers attacked the fort and retook the compound. This time the Union forces relinquished possession of Fort Proctor/ Beauregard. Once again, the Wisconsin 17th Infantry Regiment came back to the fort to attack the Confederates on September 12, 1863. The battle lasted a couple of days, and the Union forces retreated once more.

The infantry regiment tried again to rally and force the Confederates out of Fort Proctor. Some of their men were killed and tossed into Lake Borgne. Shell Island was much harder to capture than the Union forces thought. The Wisconsin 17th Infantry Regiment retreated one more time. The regiment was called away to fight in other areas of the war, leaving the fort open for capture. Later in the year, the regiment came back to Fort Proctor to attack on July 12, 1864.

The fort is still connected to a small piece of land but is accessible only by boat. The fort was built along the Renaissance style and is significant to the history of Louisiana because of its architecture and engineering techniques. Only one building of Fort Proctor is left on less than one acre of land. Completely surrounded by the river, it remains standing as a symbol of a violent past. The outer walls of the moat are all that keeps the Ouachita River from totally destroying what is left of the fort.

Fort Proctor is located on the shore of Lake Borgne in St. Bernard Parish. Visitors must rent boats to get to the old fort today. However, they must stay in their boats and must not go swimming near the fort. The solders who remain on guard do not like visitors to the island.

35

FORT JACKSON

The legend of the "blood orange" began at Fort Jackson. A young officer stationed at the fort often traveled across the river to visit a young lady. One night, he was late returning to Fort Jackson. The commander reprimanded him for being late and for seeing the woman he considered a prostitute. The officer told his young recruit that he had "to learn to obey orders and quit running with the river sluts."

Resentment raged in the young enlisted man. The subsequent argument resulted in the court-martial of the young man. He was executed by a firing squad at Fort Jackson the day after the trial. Where the young man fell and died, apparently someone had dropped some orange seeds. Within a year, a tree grew from those blood-stained seeds. When the tree was old enough to bear fruit, the inside of the oranges were found to be "streaked with blood and extra sweet."

Locals believe that the young man truly loved the lady he had visited. They further believe that the blood from his body soaked into the orange seeds. The blood he shed is what caused the reddening of the flesh of the oranges that grew on that tree. According to local legend, his love for the girl was so strong that he gave his life for her love, and that is why the blood orange is so sweet.

Some visitors to Fort Jackson have seen a young soldier standing in front of the wall at the fort. He stands there with a blindfold over his eyes and his hands tied behind his back. Suddenly rifle fire blasts through the air, and blood stains the young man's uniform. He begins to fall as his knees buckle. Before he hits the ground, he vanishes, but the blood from his wounds soaks into the ground where he stood. The legend of the blood orange lives on at Fort Jackson.

Ghosts of other soldiers who fought and died at Fort Jackson have also been reported. Corporal Morris still stands guard over Fort Jackson. Morris was killed while guarding the bastion at the fort late one night in April 1863. His body was cut in two by a shell. Killed on duty, as many men were, Morris now roams the bastion, finishing his shift.

Alaina drove out to Fort Jackson for a walk late one evening, as was her habit. She was met by a young corporal dressed in period costume. She thought this was odd, because she usually knew when there was to be a reenactment day at the fort. She questioned the young man, but he only motioned her onto the fort grounds with a polite salute. As she pressed on to the museum, she turned to look behind her. The soldier was gone. As she approached the walls of the fort, she saw the young corporal up on the bastion. From out of nowhere, bullets whizzed through the air. Alaina ducked close to the wall, startled when she saw half of the young corporal's body lying next to her. She reached out to touch his eyes to close them. She shut the man's eyes, and he turned to dust and faded away. Alaina ran to her car and left the fort. She didn't return for a long time.

Other soldiers seen roaming the grounds of Fort Jackson include several enlisted men of Company E and a man named Peter Clark of the 1st Louisiana Regiment of Artillery. Clark is usually seen around seven o'clock in the evening, about the same time he was hit by a shell and killed. In the same battle that went on for several days, the walls of Fort Jackson sustained considerable damage.

The lower Mississippi Delta was easily accessible to anyone, including enemies of the state, and although Fort St. Philip had been built to protect the settlers, they felt one fort wasn't enough. Louisianans needed stronger forts to protect them from the Spanish. General Andrew Jackson was instrumental in convincing the secretary of war of the need for another fort.

Fort Jackson wasn't the first fort to be built on the west side of the river. Timber breastworks have been identified dating to the 1700s. References to a fort at Plaquemines Bend dates back to 1746, when the French were in Louisiana. Carondelet, governor of Louisiana, ordered Fort St. Felipe (Fort St. Phillip) to be built in 1792, but he wanted it on the east banks of the river. He had named it Fort Burbon. This fort was the cornerstone of the Louisiana forts in the area. Fort Burbon was destroyed by a hurricane in 1795, leaving room for Fort Jackson to be built. The War of 1812 showed the need of a major fortification because the other forts proved to be highly vulnerable.

The building of Fort Jackson began in 1822. The construction crews built the fort in a pentagon with walls twenty-five feet above water level. It had a wide moat surrounding it. The walls were made of red brick, twenty feet thick. Foundations for the guns were strengthened with red and gray granite. The two casements facing the river were built to hold eight guns each. Barracks to house five hundred men were in a diagonal pattern in the center of the fort.

Fort Jackson sits on a foundation of three layers of cypress logs. These logs have two-by-four cypress boards stacked on top of them. The two-by-fours were used to level the foundation and were rendered airtight when submerged in water. Construction was finally finished about ten years later at a cost of $554,500.

Another ten years passed before the fort was garrisoned. At this time, President Tyler declared Fort Jackson a military reservation. At the onset of the Mexican War, Fort Jackson had to be ready at a moment's notice. In 1846, Louisiana's Governor Johnson ceded the Fort Jackson lands to the federal government. The fort was not used during the Mexican War. Much like other forts in the line of defenses guarding New Orleans, Fort Jackson had only a few soldiers at a time until the beginning of the Civil War. In 1861, the state seized the fort from the United States.

On April 18, 1862, Admiral David Farragut brought the federal fleet within striking distance of the twin forts. Through four days of bombing, the gunners on the ships besieged the forts. Although the Confederates fought back, they did little damage to the ships, which slipped past the forts to take New Orleans. The mastery of the Mississippi River belonged to the Union as of April 29, 1862.

After the Civil War, Fort Jackson wasn't forgotten as were many other defenses. The fort was used at one time for a prison. Later it was a training base. In 1898, the Spanish–American War raged, and Fort Jackson, modernized and repaired, was equipped with larger guns.

Fort Jackson was used again during World War I. The training base established there was Fort Jackson's last active facility. After this, in 1927, the fort was declared surplus property and sold to Mr. and Mrs. H. J. Harvey of New Orleans. The Harveys later donated Fort Jackson to the Parish of Plaquemines. Both Fort Jackson and its sister fort, Fort St. Philip, were designated as national historical monuments in 1960.

In 1961, restoration programs for the fort began. First, laborers built a levee to ring the fort and protect it from water damage. An automatic pumping station was installed. The mountains of slush and unwanted reptiles were then removed by prison labor. An access roadway was built to the fort, and at the end of the road, crews also constructed a three-hundred-square-foot parking area. Repairs to the walls and the guns and gun placements were restored. Workers also fixed the bridges and walkways across the moats and drains.

In order to add to the beauty of the fort, two multicolored fountains were installed on the turrets where the Spanish-American gun placements rested at one time. A subsurface lighting system and wrought-iron pickets were later installed. Grass has been planted and now covers the grounds of Fort Jackson.

Visitors and tourists are welcomed to Fort Jackson through an arch dedicated by the citizens of Plaquemines Parish to Judge Perez for his work in restoring the fort. Everyone is welcome to view permanent relics and tour the fort and the souvenir exhibits. To reach Fort Jackson, drive to the Intersection of State Highway 23 and Judge L. H. Perez Drive in Plaquemine Parish.

Visitors to Fort Jackson may be able to witness a firing squad. Fort Jackson had many deaths reported in the 1800s. Some of those men still roam the grounds.

36

FORT ST. JOHN

While visiting the ruins at Fort St. John, Dixie was confronted by five soldiers being ordered by an officer. The men seemed to be suffering from some sort of illness. The profuse sweating of the men concerned her. When she tried to help them, they shook their heads and backed away. The atmosphere around the men was terribly hot. The heat emanated from their thin, sweating bodies. She wrinkled her nose at the sickly stench coming from them. Only one thing could cause that odor: a fever. None of them stayed in her presence for long, but she saw them several times during her tour of the fort. One of the soldiers constantly mumbled. Dixie thought he wanted a drink of water. At one point, she offered him her water bottle. The man faded into the brick wall.

Dixie saw the officer roaming among the ruins without the other soldiers. Judging from his uniform, she thought he must have been a captain. The officer paced back and forth in front of the wall of the fort. He had his hands clasped behind his back. He kept his head lowered, as if he were thinking. The entire time she watched him, he mumbled quietly to himself.

The first time he appeared in front of her, she saw a flash of light move quickly to her side. She shivered at the memory of the coldness she felt at the precise time he showed up in front of her. She believes that the five soldiers are still guarding the entrance to Lake Pontchartrain at Fort St. John. The captain remains to lead his men in guarding against British invasion.

At the mouth of Lake Pontchartrain, guarding New Orleans and Bayou St. John, stands the remains of Fort St. John. The original fort was built around 1708 by the French. The fort guarded the mouth of the lake to protect the commercial trade and resident settlers, as well as for military purposes.

The French kept possession of Fort St. John until the late 1750s. In 1748, Governor Vaudreuil sent troops to the fort at the mouth of Bayou St. John to help protect the settlers from the Indians. Several small forts popped up along the lake shores to protect the settlers as well, but Fort St. John was the largest. Vaudreuil sent word to France that a hurricane had hit and done extensive damage to the fort in 1750. All of the buildings were reported damaged, and money was needed to rebuild, but no money was ever sent. The fort was abandoned by the French.

Fort St. John was claimed by the Spanish in 1765. They found the fort in need of repair. The Spanish officials took no action to repair anything at the fort.

Captain Henry Gordon of the Spanish army reported on Fort St. John a year later. He referred to the fort as a blockhouse at the mouth of the Bayou St. John. The twelve men he encountered guarding the fortress were of both French and Spanish descent. After reading Gordon's report, Governor Ulloa arrived to inspect the fort, accompanied by several French officers. The governor discovered that it had only small cannons in place. He then reported to his superiors that the little wooden fort at the mouth of the bayou was guarded by leftover cannons of poor quality iron and was virtually worthless for protection.

According to Governor Ulloa in another report to Spain, the British abandoned their forts along the lower Mississippi River in the early 1770s. He thought that, in return, he should reduce the troop count at Fort St. John, which then had only eight men left to defend its grounds. Many were of the opinion that the little log fort built on a shell base could easily fall to capture by the enemy. Thomas Hutchins of the British Navy felt that the fort could be penetrated with cannons mounted on shoal boats. He reported twelve soldiers guarding the area in 1773. The commander was a sergeant, with one subordinate, a corporal.

From 1773 to 1778, the troop list was reduced to eight men. About the same time, Governor Galvez reported to his superiors that a British vessel had fired on a Spanish schooner on the lake. He didn't figure the small fort could defend itself or the lake. The British vessel was able to stay out of the fort's cannon range. Knowing the fort was so poorly equipped, the British sent schooners of troops past the fort to Manchac many times but never fired on the fort. They were disguised and traveled at night in order not to be discovered.

In 1779, the fort, sometimes referred to as San Juan del Bayo, was reconstructed. At this time the name was changed to "Spanish Fort." In 1808, the Americans took possession of the fort and officially renamed it Fort St. John.

The fort was once described as "irregular" in shape. It consisted of nothing but boards on strong pillars at the lakeside, both inside the fort and outside. The boards, several inches apart, were filled with a dirt and shell mixture. This mixture was used to form a parapet approximately one-and-one-half-foot thick. The much stronger land side included embrasures for a battery. Even though the fort could prevent small craft from passing up the bayou, it was still vulnerable. The lakeside of the fort was open, giving enemy troops an opportunity to land and attack the fort from the rear.

Some officials felt that fortifying the Rigolets would render Fort St. John useless. However, there were those who held to the belief that Fort St. John could continue to serve Louisiana and its major port, New Orleans. Joseph Vinache was one of the men who believed in Fort St. John. With its eight-foot wood and earthen walls, Fort St. John represented protection at the mouth of the bayou. Vinache took inventory of the fort in 1795 in order to do some repair work. The wood-framed barracks had seven-foot walls. The powder magazine, a twelve-foot-square construction of brick, needed roof work on top of its eight-foot walls. The barracks and kitchen chimneys needed attention as well. The level of the fort was raised approximately three feet, but the new height didn't help. The north wind continued to blow mercilessly through the interior. Regardless of its disrepair, a half-pay officer was placed in command of the fort with twenty-five soldiers under his command.

After taking possession of New Orleans in December 1803, U.S. General James Wilkinson sent more troops to Fort St. John. The fort continued to be manned from that point until it was abandoned in 1821.

Reconstruction on the fort began in 1808 under Wilkinson's supervision. A new fort was built on the same site as the little wooden fort. The old wooden fort was covered in bricks. A year later, in May 1809, all work at Fort St. John was stopped. Only one battery had been completed, with no barracks, at a cost of $40,000. Later that year, in October, plans were resumed for construction at the fort. By March 1810, a barbette on an arc facing the lake, with embrasures for guns inside, officer's quarters, a barracks, a powder magazine, a kitchen, and a guard house were completed as ordered. In January 1811, the guns were still not mounted on the barbette.

After a very hot, sticky summer, five men, including three officers, posted at Fort St. John died of yellow fever in August 1811. Eight men remained at the fort until war was declared in 1812. Shortly after the declaration, a hurricane hit Louisiana, damaging many of the forts, including Fort St. John. This called for more plans of reconstruction. More changes were proposed. The main addition was a moat surrounding the fort. The other changes planned for the fort were tossed aside when funds were discontinued in the spring of 1813.

General Andrew Jackson sent twenty-one men to the fort in 1814, including three officers. They were enlisted for service with the 7th U. S. Infantry Regiment. A short time later, the British invasion fleet arrived. Upon the arrival of the British, more troops were sent to Fort St. John. Major Daniel Hughes was placed in command. At the same time, Captain Zacheus Shaw and his artillery company joined other troops at the fort. In January 1815, Shaw died at the fort. He left two lieutenants in command of the thirty-nine troops from the 4th Regiment of the Louisiana Militia to guard the area.

With a total of sixty men under his command, Hughes and his officers guarded mostly British prisoners being sent to Natchez. Hughes described his men as a "motley crew." The garrison was formed from several units. They were drilled on guns until, in his opinion, they would make a good accounting of themselves.

Upon arrival of the British fleet, American officials figured Fort Petite Coquilles would fail and Fort St. John would have to take on the British attack. However, the overestimation of the Petite Coquilles fort led the British down the road to Bayou Bienville, robbing Fort St. John of its moment of glory.

From 1814 until 1821 when the fort was abandoned, there were several commanders. The last was Lieutenant Schmuck. In 1823, several officers requested the use of Fort St. John to train troops. Shortly afterward, the property was sold to a private citizen, Harvey Elkins.

In the latter part of the nineteenth century, "Spanish Fort" was used as a gathering place and picnic area for citizens. Children and adults swam in the lake and entertained themselves in the old fort.

Nothing but a brick wall protrudes from the levee of Bayou St. John. The fort still guards the residents across the street. The site of the fort is now part of the City Park of New Orleans. An exchange of property took place in December 1937 to make the fort part of the park. The site for Fort St. John and the park are within the city limits, on the left bank of Bayou St. John. It is east of Beauregard Avenue, only a short distance from Robert E. Lee Boulevard.

Like Dixie, visitors to the Fort St. John site may be able to confront the spirits of the captain and enlisted men who died at the fort. Diseases instead of bullets often took lives prematurely. The apparitions are not afraid to show themselves, but they seem to be considerate enough not to come too close to visitors for fear of contaminating them.

37

FORT PETITE COQUILLES

Fishermen on Lake Pontchartrain often see the ruins of Fort Petite Coquilles. Captain Newman and his men are seen during heavy storms. Those men fought no battles, but they continue to guard the lake and New Orleans from invasion. They march on water near the foundations of the old fort. When the water of the lake is clear, the foundations can be seen seven or eight feet under water. When the spirits of Captain Newman and his garrison appear, the winds are calm and the fish do not bite.

Both the foundation of the fort and the foundation of the hospital built directly on top of the fort's foundation are visible. The hospital had been added in the 1840s after the fort was abandoned. Often the spirits of those who died at the hospital roam the banks of the lake near the ruins. Moans of men in pain can be heard from time to time. Smells of gangrenous flesh are caught in unsuspecting nostrils. Bloody bandages have floated to the surface of the water simply to disappear when anyone tried to retrieve them.

A gentleman who fishes the lake regularly has, on occasion, heard someone playing a violin near the banks of the lake. The haunting strains of music waft over the foundation ruins of the fort and out onto the lake. The birds quit singing and listen to the beautiful songs played by the spirit. The same man smells bacon cooking during the wee hours of the morning when he is on an all-night fishing trip. The first time this happened he looked for early-rising campers, but at two in the morning there was no cooking going on in the area of Fort Petite Coquilles. These leftover sounds and smells don't go unnoticed by any who are in the Rigolets Pass.

Governor Carondelet suggested in 1792 that a fort be constructed at the Rigolets at the Cattle Ranch of Maxent. He felt this location would protect New Orleans. Again in 1794, Carondelet made the same plea for a fort on the bluff or Height Coquilles. The bluff he spoke of was a shell mound about two hundred yards east of where Fort Petite Coquilles was built on a shell bank.

In 1810, General Hampton suggested a change in the boundaries of the fort because the site was in Spanish territory. General Wilkinson, who took over command from General Hampton late in 1812, eventually hired Bartholomew Lafon to draw up a plan for a new fort. Lafon was also put in charge of the construction of Fort Petite Coquilles.

Wilkinson then began erecting batteries to protect the city. In December of 1812, he ordered the construction of Fort Petite Coquilles just south of the Pass Rigolets. Wilkinson felt that Fort Petite Coquilles was instrumental in preventing the British from taking New Orleans in the War of 1812, and said there was only about two months' work needed for Fort Petite Coquilles to be completed. But construction was halted in 1813 because of lack of funds.

About sixty men were stationed at the fort in 1814. These men were members of Captain Francias Newman's Artillery Company. Captain Newman and his men were at the fort throughout the British invasion. Later in 1814, General Jackson ordered that Newman was to give his full attention to the fortification of Fort Petite Coquilles.

The day after the British captured some American gunboats on Lake Borgne, General Jackson, who was camped within a few hours' ride of the fort, decided that Fort Petite Coquilles was of little importance when it came to protecting the Pass Rigolets and sent word to Newman to only defend the post until it and its men were safe. He further ordered that Newman was to blow up the fort if it came under attack and he had to retreat. The next morning after Jackson sent the first order, he sent the second order in which he expressed his hope that Newman hadn't abandoned the fort as yet. Newman was to hold the fort longer than he was told at first. Jackson told Newman in yet another letter the following day, that a company of men was being sent to help defend the fort. A unit of about seventy mariners was sent to Fort Petite Coquilles on the fourth day, after the initial order to destroy the fort.

Later in 1814, the British made a lame attempt to take control of Fort Petite Coquilles, but upon further scrutiny they felt the fort was too strong to attack. At the time the British attempted the seizure, only about seventy regular artillery men garrisoned the fort. According to British reports, the fort appeared to be too well armed and the officer in charge of the English troops feared the loss of too many lives. Only after the British left Louisiana did Jackson send more supplies and an engineer to the fort.

General Jackson sent a company of the 2nd Infantry Regiment of about twenty artillerymen in April 1815. Later in September, the 7th Infantry garrisoned at Fort Petite Coquilles, and then in November the 1st Infantry was at the fort as well. Captain John Jones was commander. In the same year, General Jackson also asked the government for more money for repairs to the fort and asked that it be considered important to New Orleans's defense. Colonel Thomas Jesup agreed with General Jackson. As commander of the Army Department of New Orleans he ordered that Fort Petite Coquilles be repaired. However, he had his own plans for a brand-new fort. He delayed following Jackson's orders because he figured to carry out those plans.

In 1816, Jackson sent more artillerymen to the fort. Fort Petite Coquilles had several commanders who answered to General Jackson. Between 1816 and 1824 there were only forty-five men at the fort, and post reports were few and far between. Fort Petite Coquilles was abandoned after the new fort planned by Jessup was completed.

Later, in the 1840s, a hospital was built whose foundation rested directly on top of the Fort Petite Coquilles foundations. The hospital was also included as part of the new fortress. It was used during the Civil War for soldiers wounded in nearby battles. With medical supplies in short supply, the wounded often died at the hospital.

The fort's foundations are all that can be seen when the water of the lake is clear. The foundations of the hospital and part of the fort's foundation can also be seen above the water line near the banks of the lake. The Fort Petite Coquilles site is on the west side of U.S. Highway 90 about three-fourths of a mile west of the Fort Pike State Park.

Near the banks of Lake Pontchartrain, smells of infection and gangrene permeate the vicinity. There among the fish and foundations of the old fort and hospital, spirits walk on top of the water while fishermen try their luck.

38

FORT ST. PHILIP

The crashing sound of wood being bombed echoes off the banks of the Mississippi River in the early morning hours. On the river, shadowy figures of wooden ships can be seen belching flames from transparent cannons. Night visitors claim to have seen burning steamboats and rafts. The river burns, and smoke fills the atmosphere as visitors to Fort St. Philip look on.

Anyone who has been to the fort can see the damage done by the shells of the fatal attack led by David Farragut on April 18, 1862. Men from both sides of the war died in the bombardment. Many of these men still linger around the fort today.

Hank, a fisherman who likes to drop his line on a regular basis, never tries to fish in the latter part of April. "There's no need; the fish won't bite at all." Any other time of year, he has no trouble catching some kind of fish from the river. The first time he experienced the ghosts of Fort St. Philip, he was out in his boat one evening and tossed his hook into the water. The bobber went under just as if a fish had taken hold of the hook. Reeling in his catch wasn't an easy task. He had caught a body. He dragged it to his boat, and just as he reached to pull it into the boat; the body disappeared into thin air. That catch put new meaning to the words, "the one that got away."

Hank didn't panic. He tried to find the body again. He dove in the water and went under several times searching the depths of the river, but there was nothing. He thought about contacting the police, but as soon as he got back into the boat, the body reappeared and bumped the side of his craft. Again, he reached to retrieve the body. This time he was successful and pulled the body on board. The uniform of a soldier lay in the bottom of the boat, but only the uniform. Hank stared at the wet clothing, and it began to smoke and slowly dissolved into nothing.

Shrieks of drowning men come from the river depths. Cries from men shouting about being scalded by boiling water from burning steamships fill the air. The scream of these men pierce the night and the sky lights up as if the river is on fire. Hank hears the men shouting for help. They cry about the hot water. The first time this happened, Hank's feet began to feel hot as he sat in his little pirogue. He started to row to the shore, and one of the oars splashed water on his face. The water was scalding hot. Hank had a couple of red spots on his face where the water hit him.

Hank saw eerie lights dance along the crumbled walls of Fort St. Philip as darkness enveloped the river. He saw soldiers swimming in the river after midnight. He tried to talk to some of them, and they vanished. Soldiers floundered in the water as if seeking refuge, but no one could help them. Hank watched as the spirits churned the water with frantically moving arms and legs, and then the water turned red with blood and death at Plaquemines Bend.

Fort St. Philip has been known by other names: Feunte San Felipe de Placamines, Fort Plaquemines, and Fort at Plaquemine Bend. Plans for the fort, whatever it was called, began during the mid 1700s with both the Spanish and the Americans. Fort St. Philip was built across from a sister fort to create crossfire to defend New Orleans. The French government foresaw a major problem in the marshland on both sides of the river, and so did nothing about fortifying the area. The Spanish, however, felt the river needed to be fortified. Governor Miro projected plans for a battery in 1787. The plans called for enclosing a long side that faced the river curve. It would have a large redan at the center of its grounds and a demi-bastion at the end of that V-shaped projection. There would be embrasures for fourteen large cannons and twenty-four smaller ones. This was supposed to be done for a cost of $37,000. The Spanish began placing the battery for Fort St. Philip at the Plaquemines in 1790, but work in other areas of the state took precedence over Fort St. Philip.

Two years later, Governor Carondelet felt moving an older fort to the Plaquemines was necessary. Preliminary work began in 1790 with fourteen convicts and a few soldiers doing the work. The work done on the fort included, instead of a curved front, a square bastion that jutted out on each end. Historians say the fort looked as though it had horns. Giving the fort an irregular shape were a large redan on the downriver side and a small redan on the gorge side.

The fort was not completed by 1793 as Carondelet had wanted. He asked his superiors for another hundred men to finish the work at the fort. They needed to give more defense work to the back of the fort. The workers had dug a ditch and placed stakes, or palisades, in the ditch. The men hauled in enough dirt to raise the rampart, the middle bulwark, and the redans seven feet on the parapets. This was no easy task and took a long time. Six feet of dirt, when dried and packed down, measured only two feet. After all this work was done, Don Felix Truddeau was appointed commander. His garrison included one captain, one lieutenant, four sergeants, seven corporals, and thirty-eight enlisted men. Carondelet considered Fort St. Philip complete on May 13, 1793.

After all the hard labor of building Fort St. Philip, a hurricane hit and raged over the fort for more than twenty-four hours in August of the same year. The masonry wall of the fort and several trees acted as a windbreak for the fort, but the parapets were totally ruined. The fort's powder magazine was filled with mud. The carriages holding the cannon were overturned and destroyed. The moat was filled with broken trees and brush. The worst part of the destruction was the loss of life. Eleven of the men at the fort were drowned in the storm.

Military representative Guillemard directed the repairs on Fort St. Philip. The foundation repairs on the fort consisted of a lattice work of six-by-six posts, four inches apart and layered with two-inch-thick boards between the layers. Other repairs included a back rampart made of dirt. The dirt came from the twenty-foot-wide ditch that was also twelve feet deep. Twelve-foot stakes were placed along the ditch. Inside the walls of Fort St. Philip were two barracks to house three hundred men, a powder magazine, and a commander's quarters. A levee was built to extend five hundred yards at the north side of Fort St. Philip. The only entrance to the fort was a drawbridge.

A garrison at the fort included a captain and a hundred men. These men were rotated monthly. Officials kept at least one hundred convicts at the fort year round to keep the fort walls repaired. The walls would crack from the instability of the land beneath the fort, and had to be maintained.

In 1794, colored militia were sent to Fort St. Philip to keep any enemy from anchoring and attacking from below the fort. That same year, a hurricane struck the fort again. The high winds carried away the glacis and dumped about six feet of water in the sailants of the fort. Damage to the fort was extremely heavy.

A plan of Fort St. Philip showed twelve embrasures to hold large enough guns to prevent ships from attacking the front of the fort. The plans also showed a large barracks, three other buildings, and a powder magazine. Until the United States took possession of Louisiana in 1803, Fort St. Philip was at a standstill with Don Pedro Favrot as its commander. On December 23, 1803, General Wilkinson ordered Captain Cooper to be ready to defend Fort St. Philip at a moment's notice. The British were threatening an invasion that never came to Fort St. Philip.

After several commanders held office at the fort, finally, in 1808, work to make improvements began. Construction was completed in 1810. The old fort was merely a foundation for the new fort. A bastion of the old fort was repaired, but that was all that was used. The fort laborers built new walls of brick around and over the old fort walls. In February the work had begun, and by August, the 110 workers nearly died in the heat. A shortage of money and bad weather caused repairs to take a year longer than expected.

The walls of Fort St. Philip were doubled with twelve feet of dirt between the four-foot-thick walls. Despite all this, another hurricane in 1812 wreaked havoc on the fort. Upon hearing of this disaster, General Wilkinson sent workmen and materials from Natchez to the fort via steamboat. He hired Bartholomew Lafon to come up with a new design for a new compound.

With a British invasion a probability, Major General Andrew Jackson became responsible for Fort St. Philip in 1814. Upon arrival of several British ships, General Jackson ordered work to be stopped on a new battery and the materials to be brought back to Fort St. Philip. Jackson sent Major Overton to command the fort with a garrison of several companies and regiments.

In preparation for the expected attack by the British, all combustible materials were taken from inside the fort. In the second week of January 1815, the British fired approximately one thousand shells into the fort's walls. The Americans received shells for their larger guns that same day and returned fire on the enemy. After the battle was over and the British had left, the casualties were counted. Two men had been killed and seven wounded. This battle proved what Governor Carondelet and General Jackson both believed: Fort St. Philip was the key to the defense of New Orleans.

For the next fifteen years, there were at least twenty different commanders at Fort St. Philip. One of those men was Brevet Major Enoch Humphrey, who was in charge of Company B of the 4th Artillery and Company E of the 1st Infantry. The major died and was buried at Fort St. Philip in 1826.

By 1835, Fort St. Philip was badly in need of repair. The cannon carriages were rotten and falling apart. The downward slope (the glacis) from the fort to the river was damaged by the flowing river. Trees were growing inside the fort. Some of the structures could be used to rebuild and repair the fort, but the main gate and the drawbridge had to be replaced. Money for repairs, however, was not set aside until 1840. Between 1840 and 1857, the government appropriated $250,000. For repairs and the extension of Fort St. Philip. P. G. T. Beauregard supervised the reconstruction of the fort.

A lack of funds caused construction to be discontinued in December of 1858. Beauregard stayed on at the fort until 1861, when Governor Moore seized all federal installations. He sent Captain Henry St. Paul to the fort. There St. Paul found a civilian in charge of the fort, and the seizing of the property went off without a hitch. From January 16, 1861, there were many more commanders at Fort St. Philip. One was Captain Miles T. Squires. Squires was killed while commanding an artillery battalion at the fort, under Confederacy rule for the last time.

The Confederates worked for several months getting the fort and its sister fort ready for battle. Officer Farragut of the Union Army launched an attack on the forts and between April 18, 1862, and April 28, 1862, the battle raged. The crash of splintering wood and the explosions of the ships' boilers and the fort magazines filled the air. Shrieks and cries of scalded and drowning men could be heard through the smoke-thickened air. Belching flames from the guns and burning ships caused the river to look as if it were on fire. This particular battle was confined to the Plaquemines Bend. The carnage from the river was horrible, but only two men inside the fort were

Union fleet passes Fort Jackson and Fort St. Philip on the way to invading New Orleans. Courtesy of the Daily World *and the Opelousas Chamber of Commerce.*

killed, and four were wounded. The fort didn't stop the Federal fleet, which was still intact, but they were halted for a while. The fort's surrender was due to mutiny rather than destruction by the battle.

After the Civil War, the military officials saw a need for modernizing the fort's defenses. In 1868, General William T. Sherman toured the fort and saw a demonstration of weaponry firing. Between 1872 and 1876, the fort was renovated at an expense of $213,000. Parts of the fort were demolished and reused to build the new fort walls and buildings.

During the 1880s, there were no soldiers stationed at the fort. Laborers were sent to build a new levee as well as a new wharf. There were also concrete platforms for guns built to replace the wooden ones.

As the Spanish-American War raged between 1895 and 1902, more modern guns were installed at Fort St. Philip. In 1909, the fort compound included a hospital and a barracks for sixty men at the back of the fort. Up river from the fort was a one-hundred-and-twenty-man barracks and four officer's quarters. Fourteen more buildings were added to the fort during World War I.

World War I brought the need for antiaircraft guns, and Fort St. Philip was a location for these guns. The government also placed searchlights at the fort. The crews for these guns and searchlights were stationed at Jackson Barracks in New Orleans.

A report from Major Schwing referred to Fort St. Philip in 1915; it was touted as being one of the most valuable forts in the country from a historical viewpoint. Fort St. Philip and its sister fort, Fort Jackson, were abandoned in 1922 and declared surplus. In October 1926, the guns were removed, and the fort was sold to an individual. Judge Perez of Plaquemines Parish announced that the fenced part of the fort was to be cleared. It would be used as a stockade to hold any large groups who might violate the law. There were reports of apparitional visitors to the fort at that time as well as today.

Fort St. Philip is located off Interstate Highway 23 only a few miles from its sister fort, Fort Jackson. There are only a few fishermen on the river near the fort in April. The fish won't bite while the ghosts of the men who died on the Mississippi are in the water and around the fort. Visitors to the fort can hear the shrieks of terror and maybe even feel the heat from the steamship explosion. The scalding water that emanates from the burning ghost ships heats up the bottoms of the fishing boats.

39

CAMP PARAPET

"Tours by appointment only." This statement makes visitors wonder what's going on when they arrive at the fenced-in powder magazine. A year or so ago, some visitors had arranged for a tour of the small area and were greeted by several African-American soldiers marching side by side, up and down the mound. The visitors thought the curator had staged the exhibition just for them. One of the children cried out to his mother, "Look!" As she looked where her son was pointing, she saw the marching troops fade into the setting sunlight and vanish.

Sheila and her child stood back from the group of visitors. She picked up her small son and tried to explain what they had just seen. Her son kept saying "They're ghosts, Mommy," but she didn't want to admit it to him.

As she continued to try to convince him that it was just a bunch of actors, she noticed an older gentleman standing away from the powder magazine. He looked as if he were dressed like an officer, but she didn't know the Civil War ranks. He was barking orders to the troops standing in front of him. She heard one of the solders call to him, "Officer Benjamin Crowther." He seemed to sweat profusely as he instructed the troops in their use of weaponry. She watched as he stood in the sun, sweating worse. He rubbed his face with a kerchief, and she could tell he was too hot. Suddenly he fell to his knees. Finally, he collapsed face down near the men standing in ranks. He had a heart attack and died right there on the ground. She watched as some of the men picked the officer up and carried him away. At a particular point on the grounds, the officer and the men carrying him all faded into the fence surrounding the powder magazine.

Camp Parapet, a breastworks fortification, was planned to protect New Orleans from a Union attack. In August of 1861, work began on the battery. Camp

Parapet was known by several different names. One of those names was Fort John Morgan. This was to honor the heroic young Confederate from Kentucky, John Hunt Morgan.

John Morgan was one of the South's most illustrious commanders. After losing his dear wife to illness, he threw himself into the war with a vengeance. He thought he had nothing left to live for, but he made a name for himself in the war. He was well known for his hit-and-run raids against the Union troops and the railroads. He remarried a couple years later in 1863, but he continued to fight for the Southern cause. He was captured not long after his wedding and was held in a civilian prison under maximum security. He and others in his command tunneled out through the airshafts and sought civilian clothing for a train ride south. He made it as far as Greenville, Kentucky, where he was shot in the back by Federal troops.

Colonel Alfred Mouton and his regiment of Louisiana volunteers were camped at the line of fortifications near Camp Parapet until he was ordered elsewhere late in 1861. Union General Lovell reported seeing a powerful battery that extended from the river to the swamp. When Union troops took over the fort from the Confederates, they called it Camp Parapet Fortification or Camp Parapet Line. They wanted nothing to do with anything that would remind them of John Morgan.

The Union fleet appeared in New Orleans in April of 1862, causing panic among the Confederates. Troops had to be moved; weapons and ammunition had to be shipped out of the city via train. The New Orleans–Jackson and Great Northern Railroad stayed busy for several hours hauling the Rebels out of New Orleans. Because of the short time frame, given the attacking Yankees, the guns on the Parapet Line could not be removed from the battery. The Rebel soldiers spiked the cannon and burned the carriages they were mounted on. The Confederates had to skedaddle quickly or they would spend the remainder of the war in a prison camp. None of the soldiers wanted that to happen. The Confederate soldiers took everything they could carry and then some, but the big cannons had to stay behind.

Once the Union soldiers took control of Camp Parapet, they began making some improvements. There were more cannons brought to the fort, larger than the ones that were already in place at the time. The cannons that were spiked by the Confederate solders were bored out and put back into use by the Union troops. Federal soldiers remained garrisoned at the fortification until the end of the war. There were many regiments and companies of men who garrisoned Camp Parapet including the 128th of New York. One of the men from this company of volunteers, Benjamin Crowther, died of typhoid fever on March 19, 1863, at Camp Parapet.

Other units at Camp Parapet included the black regiments that started at the fort in 1862, when runaway slaves began pouring into the camp. At least a hundred people came to the fort every day looking for food and shelter. So many slaves had left the plantations around the area and come to the camp that an encampment had to be built especially for them. On the downside of the river the refugee camp was almost as large as the Camp Parapet Line. There were men and women, old and young alike. Many of the people had their children and the feeble elderly with them to make their homes outside the fortifications.

Eventually the men of the refugees were trained to fight in regiments. For a couple of years, from 1862 to 1865, the Corps d'Afrique ultimately made up eighteen armed regiments of over one thousand men per regiment.

During the battle of Port Hudson, the black troops who had trained at Camp Parapet made the difference for the Union to have victory. The Camp Parapet Regiment of Color was the first of its kind to see combat. On January 3, 1863, their commanding officers, Colonel Spencer H. Stafford, asked that his unit be allowed to fight in combat. General Banks didn't believe that the ex-slaves were fit to fight. However, as the war raged in the vicinity of Port Hudson, the 1st and 3rd Native Guard regiments were sent to provide a diversion at the ongoing battle. They were to attack the more war-ready Confederate soldiers. The troops from the black units moved forward under direct fire within two hundred yards of the Confederate's position. The Rebel artillerymen opened fire on the ex-slaves with canister, six-pound ball, and hard

Union general Nathaniel P. Banks lost the Red River Campaign, but he was victorious at Port Hudson. He was replaced at Camp Parapet. Photo courtesy of the Daily World *and the* Opelousas Chamber of Commerce.

conical shells. They threw everything they had at the black troops. The black soldiers came back time after time. After days of fighting, the Confederate soldiers on the bluff held their ground. Of the 1,080 men who went into the battle, 154 were killed or wounded. That one battle told officials in the military that the Native Guard held their own at the Battle of Port Hudson, and it was also the turning point of the war for the Union.

In 1864, the black troops were divided into three battalions, one of which was garrisoned at Camp Parapet. Lieutenant Colonel Nelson Vail commanded the Camp Parapet troops. He arranged for the African-American officers to attend night school to improve their literacy.

Three battalions of the colored troops were stationed at Camp Parapet before they were sent to Rhode Island. The last day before the camp was to close, the regiment was assembled for a dress parade. The fourteen hundred men at Camp Parapet were less five hundred of their comrades who either died or were medically discharged. After the dress parade, Camp Parapet was turned over to the First New Orleans Volunteers.

The only piece that remains of Camp Parapet is a powder magazine. It is a brick building sitting atop a mound of dirt near the river. The fenced-in powder magazine is surrounded by a residential area and can be visited by appointment only. Camp Parapet is one block from Causeway Boulevard at the end of Arlington Street.

If visitors to Camp Parapet look closely, they may be able to see Officer Benjamin Crowther training his men in the fine art of weaponry. Or they might be able to catch a glimpse of the African-American troops practicing their marching and drill skills. Some say that John Morgan visits Camp Parapet because it was originally named in honor of his heroic war record.

40

FORT DE LA BOULAYE

A handsome Frenchman stands on the east side of the Mississippi River looking out to sea. Soon he is joined by several Indians. They talk quietly among themselves for several minutes. The French soldier points to different places all around where they are standing. The Indians in turn either nod or shake their heads. Pointing here and there, the apparent leader of the Indians becomes agitated. The Frenchman says something else to them, and the Indians start slapping each other on the back and then shake his hand. They all smile and begin walking away.

Sharla puts her hand to her mouth to stifle a scream as she watches the Indians turn quickly and run at the man. One of the Indians rushes to the man and raises a tomahawk into the air and buries it in the Frenchman's back. When she reaches where she thought he fell, there is nothing but silt. The Indians had stood looking for only a moment, and then they disappeared.

Later that same day, Sharla once again saw the Frenchman in his white uniform with its red sash. His Indian moccasins protect his feet and legs, while his hat protects his face from the blazing sun. What she witnessed before was horrible, and what she was about to see was mild in comparison. The soldier stood in front of her for a few moments. Then he turned and stood in front of a large log building that had simply materialized in front of her eyes. The Frenchman moved inside and she followed. Once inside the long building, she squinted to be able to see in the darkness. She wanted to ask all sorts of questions, but her study of the spirit world had taught her to remain quiet.

As she became accustomed to the low amount of light, she saw the man standing at the other end of the room. He was surrounded by an aura of bright white light. He smiled at her and turned away. Then he vanished into the wall which, in turn, became a curtain of mist and fog. She thinks this spirit must be the lone trader who was left at Fort De La Boulaye to keep the Indians happy with the French.

This small timber construction was the first French fort within present-day Louisiana. Construction began on February 1, 1700, at the orders of the French leader Iberville. The fort has been called many different names, including Fort on the Mississippi, Fort Louisiana, Fort Iberville, and Vieux Fort, as well as Fort De La Boulaye. It was Iberville's brother Bienville who determined that the area would be suitable for a stockade. He didn't think it would be subject to flooding and even took the word of the Bayogoulas Indians on this account. They assured him the area would not overflow. Fort De La Boulaye was then built on a ridge approximately three to four feet high. It seems that the woods around the area had a lot to do with his choice as well. There were oaks, elms, and ash trees growing in abundance in the area.

The French built a powder magazine of the wood and plastered it with mud. It was eight feet square, and its mud and wooden walls measured a foot-and-a-half thick. The magazine was built approximately five feet off the ground in case flooding occurred. The only other building at the fort was supposed to be two stories tall. It was a large building with walls twenty-eight feet long.

Iberville hoped that Fort De La Boulaye would secure France's possessions in the lower Mississippi. He planned a number of cannon defenses with six larger guns. It was to be surrounded by a moat that would be twelve feet wide. After it was completed, a visitor came by and said he saw six cannons, but he thought that they were much smaller than originally planned. The cannons weren't even set up at the fort but were set up on the banks of the Mississippi River instead. Another visitor to Fort De La Boulaye said the fort was at least one-fourth of a league (three-fourths of a mile) from the river. It seemed that the nearby bayou gave the French hope for a shortcut to the Gulf of Mexico. If the shortcut worked out, they would not have to travel fifty miles over land to the mouth of the Mississippi River.

Accounts of commanders at Fort De La Boulaye differ. Bienville commanded the post until Sauvole's death in 1702. LaRonde, a marine in the French Navy, is mentioned as being a commander at the fort. Bienville wrote a letter to Pontchartrain in September of 1704, saying that St. Denis was the commanding officer at Fort De La Boulaye, with only fifteen troops.

On February 10, 1707, another letter from Bienville told Pontchartrain that the fort was being abandoned because it was too hard to get supplies.

Besides that, the Indians didn't give him the truth about the area overflowing. Bienville left one man at the fort to keep trading with the Indians. The first man left at Fort De La Boulaye alone was murdered by disgruntled Indians. He was found, with a tomahawk lodged in his back, by some of Beinville's men as they came to check on the status of the post's supplies. He had been left there to trade with the Indians just as if there were many soldiers at the fort. Bienville picked out another "volunteer" and left him at the fort. He was to have the same duties as the last man: keep trading with the Indians. Supplies would be provided on an as-needed basis.

Because the fort wasn't totally abandoned, it was kept on the trade route and used as a stopover for the travelers on the river. The soldiers kept supplies at the fort so that if they needed to restock while in the field, they could take the supplies as they needed them.

The final name of the fort has an uncertain source. Some people say it was named for Chavalier Claude Agnan Guerin de la Boulaye. More than likely, however, the name came from Louis Hyancinthe Plomier Sieur de la Boulaye. He was the inspector general for the French Navy in 1697 and went to the Antilles on an inspection tour in 1700. At one point, he inspected the fort and gave it a good report.

Several eighteenth-century maps show the fort or its ruins to be approximately fifty miles from the mouth of the Mississippi River. It is also shown on the east side of the river, although other maps show it on the west side of the river. With the shifting of the delta at the mouth of the river, either of these locations could be accurate.

In 1930, Maurice Reis, Albert Lieutenant, Gordown W. Callender, and Prescott Follett researched Fort De La Boulaye and found it was definitely on the east bank of the Mississippi River. It is about four thousand feet from the river now. The ruins sit on a ridge only two miles from Phoenix, Louisiana. The owners of Maria Plantation, the Gravelot brothers, dug a canal through the ruins of Fort De La Boulaye in 1923. There is nothing left of the small fortification of Fort De La Boulaye on the east bank of the Mississippi River mouth.

Visitors to the area can travel to the mouth of the river to see where the fort once stood. Perhaps the Frenchman will invite them into the old log building to see his world from inside the past. He may try to strike up a trade with the spirits of the Indians and let the visitors watch.

FURTHER READING

BOOKS

Casey, Powell A. *Encyclopedia of Forts, Posts, Named Camps and Other Military Installations in Louisiana 1700–1981*. Baton Rouge, LA: Claitor's Publishing Division, 1983.

Ford, James A. *Analysis of Indian Collections from Louisiana to Mississippi*. New Orleans: Department of Conservation, Louisiana Geological Survey, 1936.

Hardin, J. Fair. *Fort Jesup–Fort Selden–Camp Sabine–Camp Salubrity: Four Forgotten Frontier Army Posts of Western Louisiana*. New Orleans: Cabildo, 1933.

Marchand, Sidney A. *The Story of Ascension Parish 1800–1900*. Salem, MA: Higginson Book Company, 1995.

McGregor, Charles. *The History of the 15th New Hampshire Volunteers: 1862–1863*. Concord, NH: Ward House Books, 1900.

Roberts, Robert B. *Encyclopedia of Historic Forts: The Military, Pioneer, and Trading Posts of the United States*. New York: Macmillan, 1987.

Saxon, Lyle, Edward Dryer, and Robert Tallant. *A Collection of Louisiana Folk Tales: Gumbo Ya-Ya*. Gretna, LA: Pelican Publishing Company 1945, 1998.

Soldier of the Eighty-First Regiment Illinois Volunteer Infantry. *Experience in the War of the Great Rebellion*. Carbondale, IL: Edmund Newsome Publisher, 1880.

Townsend, Luther. *The History of the 16th Regiment of New Hampshire Volunteers*. Washington, D.C.: Ward House Books, 1897.

Wright, Carley Ruth Basco. *Entangled Web of Bayou Pierre*. Sulphur, LA: Wise Publishing, 1999.

DIARIES/JOURNALS

Johnson, Colonel Benjamin Whitfield. "Report on Fort Desperate." Confederate Soldiers of America (CSA) Collection. Baton Rouge, LA: VAAPR, Inc.

Milneer, P. M. "Fort Macomb." *Louisiana Historical Publications*, III (1913–1914).

WEBSITES

"Civil War (1861–1865)," Landry Family History. At friends.xocamp.net.

"Colonel Benjamin Whitefield Johnson," Port Hudson CSA.–Fort Desperate. At home.earthlink.net.

"Fort Beauregard History," Fort Beauregard Marina Estates. At www.fortbeauregard andmarina.com.

"Fort Massachusettes," Gulf Island Seashore. At www.nps.gov/.

"Haunted New Orleans," History of Louisiana Hauntings. At www.prairieghosts .com.

"History of Fort Jackson," Fort Jackson History. At tec.uno.edu/.

"Important Dates in Louisiana History," Louisiana Department of Economic Development. At www.crt.state.la.us/.

"Louisiana," All About Ghosts. At dawghouse.topcities.com.

"Louisiana Haunted Places," The Shadowlands Haunted Places Index. At theshadow lands.net.

"Louisiana, St. Bernard County," National Register of Historical Places. At www. nationalregisterofhistoricplaces.com.

"New Orleans Forts," Fort Livingston. At www.atneworleans.com.

Payette, Pete. "Louisiana," American Forts East. At www.geocities.com/naforts/la.htm.

"September 6, 1863, Fort Morganza," This Week in the Civil War. At www.civil week.com.

"State Historic Site, Port Hudson," Louisiana State Parks. At www.crt.state.la.us.

"Von Mueller, Louisiana," Louisiana Ghost Towns. At bwcpublishing.com.

"Wisconsin17th Infantry Regiment," Civil War Regiments Wisconsin Genealogy. At linkstothepast.com.

INDEX

ABOUT THE AUTHOR

Elaine Coleman is an award-winning author of two books, *Texas Haunted Forts* and *Texas Frontier Foods*. She lives deep in the heart of Texas, where she and her husband raise cattle and horses on the family farm. Elaine has been writing stories and researching history since she was ten years old. She draws inspiration from the history around her and also from her five grandchildren.